RANGER STORIES
TRUE STORIES FROM BEHIND THE RANGER IMAGE

*Thirty Years with the National Park Service and
the Bureau of Land Management*

MICHAEL JOHN MEYER
SUPERVISORY LAW ENFORCEMENT RANGER, RETIRED
US DEPARTMENT OF THE INTERIOR

Printed in the United States of America
ISBN 1-58385-114-3

ACKNOWLEGMENTS

The journey that has become this book was long, but fun.

There are many people I want to thank who have made that journey smoother: my parents, Henry and Elizabeth Meyer, who sometimes didn't understand the direction I took in my career, but were always supportive of me.

To Valerie and Scott who shared the adventure.

To the true believers who know that being a ranger is far more than just a job, it is a reason for being: Robert Love, Steve Stockdale, Reid Hopkins, Brian Smith, Ken Phillips, Paul Crawford, Bill Briggs, Bob Zimmer, Mike Dobson, Bryan Pittman, Larry Nicky, John Bierk, Tom Biller, William Wagers, Fred Delcamp, George Giddings, Ken Kelly, Todd Swain, Keith Lober, John McLaughlin, Matthew Wohlberg, Jerry Bronson, Mark Harris, Roger Moder, Tom Cox, Laura De La Garza, and to the many others.

To John Blachley, my best friend and colleague of thirteen years.

To Sally Allen who has loved me more than anyone else.

I also want to thank my editor, Katie Sulkowski, and publisher at Cold Tree Press, Peter Honsberger, who made this book come together.

T🌲BLE OF CONTENTS

Introduction . . . . *i*

Chapter 1 — Belonging for the First Time 1

Chapter 2 — Taking Our Chances 5

Chapter 3 — The Edge of the World 9

Chapter 4 — First Call 17

Chapter 5 — Two Times in One Day 21

Chapter 6 — Alex Christopher Ewing Was Here 25

Chapter 7 — Rescue at the Marina 29

Chapter 8 — In the Face of Change 33

Chapter 9 — "But We Are From France!" 37

Chapter 10 — Illegal Bead Sellers 41

Chapter 11 — Unforgettable Days at the Grand Canyon . 45

Chapter 12 — The Last People to See It 49

Chapter 13 — "Knives Were Involved". 57

Chapter 14 — Too Much For One Day 61

Chapter 15 — Extra Support 67

Chapter 16 — One Lucky Man 71

Chapter 17 — Not Today 75

Chapter 18 — Above the Arctic Circle 81

Chapter 19 — Sometimes When You Visit Hell,

           You Get Burnt 85

Chapter 20 — A Journey Interrupted 93

Chapter 21 — Thief of Time 99

Chapter 22 — A-Canal Water Wars 103

Chapter 23 — The Last Time 113

Chapter 24 — Prologue 115

INTRODUCTION

I am one of the truly lucky people of this world. I had the privilege to work as a ranger. Others say that they had the best job in the world, but they only say that because they never experienced life as a ranger. I spent my life not working for a corporation helping to make the CEO a richer man; instead, I was given the honor of protecting America's most important resource: its parks and public lands. I was able to protect those things which are precious to America but have no voice, and help people visit, appreciate, and use those resources. This profession gave me the most incredible and rewarding experiences. I had babies born into my hands and people die in my arms. Nothing can express the honor I felt in being able to perform those duties.

As a boy I never planned on being a ranger, though, I should have seen the direction my life was taking long before I put my first ranger hat on. I always loved being outdoors. It was one of the few places that I felt comfortable. Being outside and alone has always been a comfortable place for me. My parents were not big campers, but the few times we went camping I was so happy. I loved being outdoors as much as I liked fishing. My grandfather regularly took me fishing along San Diego Bay. As I grew older, I started exploring the many canyons that surrounded our house.

In the 1950s and 60s San Diego was still a small Navy town. I was blessed with the chance to hike and explore the many canyons that led to Mission Valley. Most of those canyons are gone now, filled in with dirt and covered by expensive homes. What lies below those homes are a young boys first adventure and contentment with an outdoor life.

While working towards my bachelor's degree in geology at San Diego State University, I got my first summer job working as a ranger for the United States National Park Service at Glacier National Park in Northwest Montana. I wasn't that interested in taking the job, but love and a new wife got me to drive the fifteen hundred miles north for a ninety-day job. My life was never the same after that summer. I loved the beauty of Glacier. I loved the camaraderie of my fellow rangers and I loved the adventure of what we were doing, protecting one of America's most precious jewels. That summer I found a direction for my life.

After graduating I worked the winters as a soils technician for different geology firms in San Diego as my wife finished her degree. During the summers, I quit to return to Glacier. When my wife was accepted into the Library of Science Masters Degree Program at the University of Arizona in Tucson, I worked as a seasonal ranger at Saguaro National Park there in Tucson.

My first permanent job with the Park Service was at Arches National Park in Utah. Although it was for only ten months of the year, it was considered permanent. After three years I became the Wildrose sub-district ranger at Death Valley National Park in California, a remote assignment which developed a different set of ranger skills. I then went to Callville Bay at Lake Mead National Recreational Area in the Mojave Desert in Nevada where heavy duty law enforcement was the main focus of the job. After four years, I moved to Lassen Volcanic National Park in

Northern California where I was the primary law enforcement ranger. I was then promoted to shift supervisor on the South Rim of Grand Canyon National Park in Arizona. The five years I spent on the South Rim were the best of my career. There, my life and work molded into one.

After those five years at the South Rim I had to make a choice both in my family life and my career. My son was getting ready to complete elementary school. Grand Canyon had an excellent grade school program with small classes and excellent teachers, but the high school program lacked direction. Also, my wife had held many different jobs over the years, but hadn't had a chance to use her skills as a librarian. When I found out the Bureau of Land Management (BLM) was expanding its ranger program and needed supervisors, I applied and got a job as a supervisory law enforcement ranger in the California Desert District working out of the Palm Springs office. This move to a new agency and bigger city was beneficial for the whole family. It allowed my son to attend a better education program and my wife to quickly get a job managing a library.

It was extremely hard leaving the Park Service. I loved being a Park Service ranger and I truly respected my fellow rangers. It was a hard day as I drove out of the gates of Grand Canyon for Palm Springs. Four ranger patrol cars surrounded my vehicle as I was escorted out of the park with full lights and sirens going just as we had done with visiting dignitaries. My eyes were full of tears as I passed through the gates for the last time. The Park Service had left a tattoo on my soul, like a faded globe and anchor on an old marine's shoulder.

At the time I worked for BLM, it had a very small law enforcement component. We had about one hundred forty rangers to cover over 278 million acres, or about 2 million acres per ranger.

Considering Yellowstone National Park is about 2 million acres in size and has a ranger force of forty, the difference is substantial. The BLM ranger force was smaller than the Library of Congress law enforcement contingence.

The small number of rangers did have its advantages in allowing for a lot of details, or assignments, to different areas of the country. I worked in Alaska above the Arctic Circle, in Utah and Colorado protecting archeology sites, in Arizona protecting the facile desert ecology from the onslaught of illegal aliens, in Montana, Idaho, and Wyoming protecting the forests from timber poachers and persons stealing oil from public lands, in Oregon patrolling the beaches protecting the snowy plover and least terns nesting grounds. There were also special details to the 1996 Olympics, Burning Man, a week-long festival that culminates in the burning of a large wooden statue in the Nevada Desert, the water rights wars on the Klamath River, and numerous details to the Imperial Sand Dunes where three hundred thousand off-roaders meet on the holidays.

The BLM Palm Springs office was one of the busiest of all the field areas. I supervised nine law enforcement rangers in Riverside and San Diego Counties. Being on the edge of a urban area, a large array of crimes were committed on public lands such as, dumping hazardous materials, committing arson, manufacturing methamphetamine in mobile labs, growing marijuana, illegal use of assault weapons, stealing and poaching endangered species, smuggling illegal aliens over the US border, trespassing closed areas. Along with those crimes we had all the assorted urban crimes such as, murder, rape, vehicle theft, and assault. For many years we led the BLM in law enforcement incidents. I worked thirteen years in the Palm Springs office and there was never a dull day.

My ranger career spanned thirty years from 1975 to 2005.

When I started, the National Park Service had limited law enforcement authority. Basically, if you had been in the military and gone through a twenty-four-hour training program, you were given a badge, citation book, and a gun to share with other rangers and told to go out and protect the resource. One of the first things I remember being told was that bad guys don't come to parks and if they do it's only at night, so don't wear your gun because it offends the visitors. I soon found that it wasn't the visitor that was offended, they usually thought we should be armed, it was the managers. Most of the superintendents and chief rangers I worked for had never done any law enforcement and had gotten into the Park Service long before the visiting public had changed. They were far more interested in protecting an image than in what was happening around the park.

That all changed with The Federal Land Policy and Management Act of 1976. For the first time ever, the Secretary of the Interior was given the power to establish a law enforcement ranger force with specific standards and training which professionalized the law enforcement programs for the National Park Service and the Bureau of Land Management. It gave both agencies their first true law enforcement power which meant perpetrators would face consequences for illegal crimes. Both the National Park Service and the Bureau of Land Management are agencies within the US Department of the Interior. The main mission of the Park Service is to preserve and protect the public lands while the BLM manages the use of 262 million surface acres of America's public lands stretching over twelve western states.

The journey to law enforcement was not an easy one and still is not. Since it is not the primary mission of the Park Service or the Bureau of Land Management, the programs are controlled by non-law enforcement managers. These managers have other responsibilities and law enforcement is usually placed on the back burner. Those of us that took our job seriously, and were proud of what we did, were often criticized.

I can remember attending a Park Service staff meeting once where I was told I had to take my defensive equipment belt off before I could enter the room. The reason given was that it offended the sensibilities of some other employees. I pointed out to the manager that my position description stated that my primary job function was law enforcement and wearing my equipment belt was part of my uniform. I kept my belt on and attended the meeting. I got some stares from one or two employees and I stared back, but no one said anything about my wearing the belt again.

Another incident occurred when I applied for the position of chief ranger at Chiricahua National Monument in southern Arizona. During a phone interview with the superintendent, that I could tell wasn't going well, he stopped the interview and said that I was certainly qualified for the job, but there was no way he was going to hire anyone who had worked at Lake Mead. He stated that people who worked at Lake Mead had the wrong attitude about the Park Service.

These prejudices against law enforcement became less as the years went by, but still exist. As long as you have managers who have never preformed law enforcement duties in control over the program, you will have a program that is limited in what it can accomplish.

The following stories are true and are taken from my daily life as a ranger. Some of the names have been changed, but those who were there will know who they are. These events track my career over a thirty-year time span and I hope show some of the progression that law enforcement has taken in the Department of the Interior.

To my readers, I hope you will be entertained and learn something from these stories written by a man who was a ranger first and a writer second — this book is a combination of the reporting style I used for my job and the journaling I did for my own personal reflections later. What you have here are the uncensored stories of life as a law enforcement ranger.

It is not the critic that counts, not the man who points out how the strong man stumbles, or where the doer of deeds could have done better. The credit belongs to the man who was actually in the arena. Whose face is marred by the dust, sweat and blood. Who strives valiantly, who errs and comes short again and again. Who knows the great enthusiasms, the great devotions. Who spends himself on a worthy cause. Who at best knows in the end the triumph of high achievement. Who at worst, if he fails, at least fails while daring greatly. So that his place shall never be with those cold and timid souls who know neither victory nor defeat.

— Theodore Roosevelt

RANGER STORIES

TRUE STORIES FROM BEHIND THE RANGER IMAGE

Thirty Years with the National Park Service and
the Bureau of Land Management

MICHAEL JOHN MEYER

SUPERVISORY LAW ENFORCEMENT RANGER, RETIRED
US DEPARTMENT OF THE INTERIOR

CHAPTER ONE
BELONGING FOR THE FIRST TIME

Glacier National Park, Kalispell, MT

"Jake's down, I'm down!" The radio fell silent and then suddenly came alive with everyone trying to talk at the same time. After the initial burst of radio traffic, little bits of information started to come across.

"Was that Lloyd?"

"I think they're at Amy's Bar with a warrant."

"Dispatch, do you have a location?" I started running towards the Rising Sun Campground Ranger Station. As I approached the station, Chuck came barreling around the corner in the small white Ford pick-up truck. I jumped into the passenger seat banging my knees on the dashboard. We could now hear the echo of sirens across the valley and the steady voice of Roger as he sped towards Amy's Bar just outside the park in St. Mary's. Lloyd, the St. Mary's supervisory ranger, had been trying to serve a federal warrant on Amy for the last month. She had a habit of lifting up the fence railing between the Blackfoot Reservation and Glacier National Park and letting her horses graze on the sweet grass inside the park. The railing was always replaced and she claimed the horses had just "appeared" on the park's side. She had been given numerous citations and now the federal magistrate had issued a mandatory appearance warrant. Lloyd had been trying to give the warrant to Amy for the last two weeks, but every time he went by her bar, there were numerous local pick-up trucks parked outside. To avoid a confrontation, Lloyd waited until Amy was by herself. Apparently, Jake and Lloyd had gone into the bar and something bad had happened.

As Chuck and I rounded the last bend and crossed the St. Mary's River, we heard Roger's controlled voice on the radio telling dispatch that he had arrived and needed all units to continue responding to Amy's.

Less than two minutes later, Chuck and I arrived and found Roger wiping blood off Jake. Jake's face was swollen beyond recognition and blood drained out of his mouth and onto the ground. Lloyd's shirt was ripped and there were fresh blood stains on it. The bend rim of Lloyd's thick glasses sat crooked across the bridge of his nose.

Chuck and I were seasonal rangers that had limited law enforcement authority. During the 1970s, the National Park Service still held the quaint notion that criminals didn't visit parks, and if they did, only under the cover of darkness. Therefore, we were not given any defensive equipment. Patrol rangers like Jake and Roger shared a .38 cal. revolver between them. So Chuck and I tried to act tough and keep the Blackfoot tribal members away from where Roger provided medical aid to Jake. Words were exchanged between the Blackfoot and me, but no physical contact occurred. I heard more sirens in the distance and silently thanked God as each time a unit arrived. Since there wasn't enough defensive equipment for each ranger, many showed up with their own personal weapons or large caliber bear management pistols and rifles. Finally, Jake was lifted into the Dodge station wagon, which served as ambulance and patrol vehicle, and Roger sped him off towards Caniston, Canada, fifty miles to the nearest hospital.

After Jake was gone, Lloyd told us the story of what had happened. After Jake finished his patrol shift, he gave Roger his gun and Lloyd picked Jake up and was going to take him home. As they approached the park exit, Lloyd tried to serve Amy the warrant. They went by the bar and found no vehicles parked in front. Since Jake had no defensive equipment, he stood outside by the door as Lloyd entered the bar. Lloyd immediately knew it was a mistake. Inside the bar numerous Blackfoot Indians were playing pool. These were some of the same people that Lloyd had either arrested or were confirmed poachers. Words were exchanged and Lloyd told them that he was only there to serve Amy with an appearance warrant and would be leaving. As Lloyd turned to face Amy at the bar, a pool ball flew through the air and hit the mirror above the bar. Lloyd turned back towards the Blackfoot just in time to see them charging towards him. At that moment, Jake was standing in the doorway and heard the noise from inside as another Blackfoot, returning from the outside pit toilet, crashed into Jake bringing him to the ground. As Lloyd struggled with the Blackfeet inside the bar, Jake was kicked mercilessly in the head until he was knocked unconscious. Lloyd finally broke free from his attackers, drew his service revolver, and backed out of the bar to protect the unconscious Jake. The Blackfoot immediately left the bar and drove off in their trucks which were parked behind the bar.

Later in the afternoon we found out that Jake had suffered numerous factures around the orbits of both eyes and had some teeth knocked out. The FBI arrived that afternoon and interviewed Lloyd. Even though Lloyd knew the identities of his attackers it took over a month before anyone was arrested, and when they were convicted and sentenced, the longest jail time given was thirty days. The park superintendent at that time wanted to keep the incident in the background and out of the press because of his desire to maintain the "good relationship" with the Blackfoot Nation. This was my first exposure to the disconnect between management personnel and those in the field. It was also the first time that I felt I belonged to a group who shared a common bond. Even though my part in the incident was minor, Chuck and I had responded to our fellow rangers in need, and that was a feeling that I wanted to keep for the rest of my life.

CH🌲PTER TWO
TAKING OUR CHANCES

Arches National Park, Moab, UT

"**K**-O-P-700-400. K-O-P-700-400." The call echoed across my living room at Arches National Park. I waited for someone from Canyonlands National Park to answer. The Park Service dispatch ended at 5:00 p.m., but I kept listening until 6:30 p.m.

This was before the days of cell phones and the only way for the remote stations to communicate was by radio. I was one of a few rangers that had a radio in their house and I kept mine on twenty-four hours a day. My first responsibility was for Arches National Park, but the system also monitored Canyonlands and Natural Bridges about 70 miles away.

The call came across the radio again. This time I heard the urgency in the caller's voice. I picked up the microphone and answered. The caller stated that one of the rangers, Jim, who lived at Needles Ranger Station, was having a heart attack. Jim was on oxygen, complaining of chest pains and they wanted the Life Flight Helicopter out of Grand Junction dispatched. I copied the vital signs they gave me and then called the hospital on the phone.

While trying to reach the right persons at the hospital, I received another call from Needles that they had just started CPR on Jim. I passed this on to the Life Flight dispatcher, but she told me that the helicopter was out of the area and unavailable. I knew that it would take an ambulance at least an hour and a half to reach Needles and then another hour and a half to get back to Moab. Three hours was just too long for someone who was in cardiac arrest.

I called Charlie, the chief ranger of Arches National Park, and we discussed our options. The only one that offered us any real hope was to try and get one of the private helicopters operators to fly us to Needles. This would break most of the Department of the Interior flight rules, since the helicopter had not been certified by the Department, but we decided to take that bureaucratic risk. I called the pilot and explained the situation. It didn't take much to get him motivated; he knew Jim and had been monitoring our radio traffic.

Within minutes, Charlie and I arrived at the helicopter just as the pilot started the rotors turning. After a quick preflight check we were airborne. The sun was just setting lighting up the cliffs along the Spanish Valley. It was a quick flight to Needles and we landed just as it was getting dark. As I unbuckled my safety harness, I commented on what a great job the pilot had done landing in such a small area next to the flag pole. The pilot squinted his eyes, looked at the pole and said he hadn't even seen it. That didn't give me the best feeling.

Charlie and I got our medical gear and ran over to Jim's trailer. There on the floor were two Park Service maintenance workers doing CPR on Jim. His skin was ashen white and you could see that his pupils were dilated. His three sons, all between the ages two and six, sat on the sofa each holding a stuffed animal. Their eyes were vacant as they stared at the scene before them. Marge, Jim's wife, grabbed me by the arm and said,

"Jim's going to be alright!" I think she said this more for her sons than for the reality around her. Marge's statement, the boy's eyes, and Jim almost dead on the floor is a moment frozen in my mind forever.

Since the helicopter had limited space, we decided to place Jim on a half backboard and lay him across the back seat of the helicopter with his knees folded. Charlie was small enough to kneel on the floor and give breaths while I bent over Jim and did chest compressions. The flight back to Allen Memorial Hospital in Moab took twenty minutes. We landed on the grass on the side of hospital and Jim was rushed inside. Charlie and I crawled out of the helicopter and sat on the grass. We were exhausted both mentally and physically.

When we got our strength back, we walked into the emergency room and saw the green sheet over Jim's body. The doctor told us that Jim had died of a massive heart attack and that there was nothing that could be done for him. I always wondered if Jim hadn't lived in such a remote location maybe his chances for survival would have been better. But this was a chance we all took when we chose to be rangers.

CHAPTER THREE
THE EDGE OF THE WORLD

Death Valley National Park, Death Valley, CA

Death Valley National Park isn't a place you think your career is going to take you to, but some times you have to pass through a place to get to where you want to be.

Death Valley was that place for me. It was 1981 and previously Jimmy Carter decided his administration wasn't going to hire any more federal employees. I had been working at Arches National Park in Utah for three years as a subject to furlough employee which meant that I worked ten months of the year and was laid off the other two months. I had all the federal benefits, but wasn't considered a full-time employee so I couldn't apply for any jobs. I wanted more responsibility and full-time employment. I was a low graded a GS-5 ranger. The employment grade for Federal employees begins with GS-1 and goes to GS-15. With a wife to support, my paycheck didn't go that far.

My interest was peaked when I saw an announcement for a GS-7 ranger job at Death Valley, California. I became really excited when I learned that they were taking applications from people who did not have full-time status. The job description included being the ranger for the Wildrose district which ran the length of the Panamint Mountains on the western side of Death Valley. The ranger would live at the Wildrose ranger station which was also on the western side of the Panamint Mountains facing Panamint Valley. This was an extremely remote location sixty miles from Furnace Creek in Death Valley and sixty-three miles from Ridgecrest California. There was no telephone service and no reliable television or radio reception. A one-cylinder generator supplied electrical power, a natural spring supplied water, and gravity supplied the force that operated the sewer system. Wildrose was not exactly the end of the world, but the edge could be seen from there.

I put in my application and hoped for the best. I made all the proper campaign calls to the chief ranger, and the district ranger expressing my interest and qualification for the position. Sixty three people applied for the job and to my amazement I was selected. I hadn't talked to Valerie, my wife, about the job details only that I had applied to Death Valley. Neither of us thought I had much of a chance with my subject to furlough status being a limiting factor. So then we were faced with having been given something that we couldn't really pass up but weren't sure we wanted. In the end, a promotion and full-time status were too important to pass up. We took the job and I promised Val that I would only be there for a short time.

After the movers unloaded our stuff at Wildrose one of them took me aside and wanted to know what I had done to be exiled to such an isolated place. He saw our beautiful stone house at Arches National Park and couldn't believe where we were now. When I told him that this was a promotion, he just shook his head and said that the Park Service certainly had some strange ideas about promotion.

When we arrived at Wildrose, a maintenance man and his wife were living there. They only lasted for three months after we got there. His wife just couldn't take the isolation. Before he transferred, however, he was able to show me how all the systems worked. So I also became the maintenance man along with my ranger duties. For the first time in my life I was completely responsible for everything that happened around me. If I didn't check the generator every eight hours we'd lose power, if I didn't keep the valves open and clear the sewer backed up, and if I didn't check the spring and keep the water line clean we had no water. We were truly on our own with our view of the edge of the world.

Valerie and I had been married six years by the time we reached Wildrose. Since Val had always worked and there were definitely no employment opportunities for her at Wildrose, we decided that this would be a great time to have a baby. To our pleasant surprise, Val quickly became pregnant.

Val was never one for eating right and exercising, but as soon as she became pregnant she changed her ways. She ate things she never would have eaten before, and she took long walks. This presented some interesting problems for me. First of all, as the pregnancy progressed, her eyesight worsened.

Many large western diamondback rattlesnakes lived around Wildrose, and as with most snakes if you leave them alone, they wouldn't hurt you. But to avoid them, you have to first see them. Usually I drove Val five or six miles above the ranger station and she walked back home. On the drive up I would point out the rattlesnakes along the road, and on my drive back down I would chase the snakes off the road. Val never saw the snakes, and I felt she was safe on her walk back down.

Sometimes park visitors saw my wife on her walks. To them, they saw this very pregnant women walking down this extremely remote road and become concerned about her well being. They tried to give her a ride or express their concern about her welfare. Val always refused the rides and told them she was alright. Numerous times I got visitors at the station expressing their concern about this crazy pregnant woman walking in the middle of the desert. I told them that she really wasn't crazy, she was just married to me.

As Valerie's due date got closer, more and more people became concerned about the birth. Other rangers brought us OB kits. Word got out to the Life Flight Helicopter and the crew made a special trip to check out the landing areas at Wildrose. They were a little concerned about having a safe landing area, so I hauled some asphalt up to Wildrose and built a small helipad.

Scott, our son, was born on October 12, 1981, two weeks over due. After a three-day stay in the hospital we brought Scott home. Valerie and I now had a three-day-old baby to take care of, sixty-three miles from the nearest town, with no telephone, and no one else to ask all the questions that new first time parents have to ask. The remoteness of our situation really hit us.

In the following weeks, several park service people came by to see our new baby. One of the first people to hold Scott, who wasn't a relative, was Gene Nunn, a Bureau of Land Management horse wrangler. At the time, Gene rounded up feral burros in the park. He acted and dressed the part of a nineteenth-century cowboy. His body and face were shaped by the years he had spent living outdoors and working with the horses he loved. He had slyly asked to hold Scott. As he picked Scott up with his harden hands, his eyes lit up and an expression of compassion and happiness filled his face as he held him. I truly felt lucky to be the father of such a magical thing.

I spent most of my days patrolling the area and doing mainte-nance. The routine gave me a sense of ownership for the area that so many rangers acquire. I read the old reports of past rangers and learned about the history of the area. One of the intriguing stories was that of the days when Charlie Manson and his gang roamed the area. Manson had been captured at Barker Ranch in the southern part of my district by Park Service rangers.

One day I had my own meeting with a member of the Manson gang. I was driving down to the edge of the park to check one of the water tanks when I saw a man and woman sitting on a motorcycle by the side of the road. I recognized the man as a local character named "Coyote" who lived in an old abandoned mining camp outside the park. The woman was middle-aged and wore full motorcycle gang leather. I asked if they needed any help and Coyote said no that they were just admiring the view. He then asked me if I knew who the woman was and I said I didn't know. He introduced her as Cathy Gillies one of "Charlie's Girls." We talked for awhile and then Coyote told Gillies to tell me about Charlie Manson and Wildrose. Gillies went on to tell how Manson really liked Wildrose and how he and Tex Watson and others had practiced their "creepy crawly" maneuvers in the ranger houses at Wildrose. As Gillies spoke I noticed the "X" scar on her forehead.

After my talk with Coyote and Gillies I returned to the station and found the dog eared copy of Vincent Bugliosi book Helter Skelter which told Manson's story. There was a picture of Gillies standing outside the Los Angeles Courthouse with an "X" curved in her forehead protesting Manson's trial. It also recounted Manson telling his gang to use the creepy crawly moves when they committed the Tate and La Bianca murders. That night then I was lying in bed I couldn't get the image of Manson and Watson crawling around this house. It didn't make sleeping all that easy.

My other major duty at Wildrose was working with the various groups who researched and removed the feral burros from the area. The burros had been left behind by prospectors during

Death Valley's mining days. They were native to North Africa and had no natural predators in the desert. Their numbers had increased at alarming rates so that by the early 1980s they were destroying most of the native habitat. The Nelson bighorn sheep had been most hard hit. The burros eat all the vegetation for miles around the natural springs which the bighorn depended on for water and food. This forced the bighorns to travel greater distances to survive during the hot summer months. The stress placed on the sheep had drastically reduced their numbers.

The burros, much like the grizzly bears of Yellowstone Park, had become synonymous with Death Valley. They looked cute and cuddly and the public loved to see them. Like the grizzly bears, the Park Service allowed the public's affection towards these animals to influence their better judgment to keep the numbers down. The result was the burro population got out of hand. Then when the bighorn sheep were placed on the endangered species list, the Park Service had to react.

It was decided that the burros had to be removed, but the Wildhorse and Burro Act of 1970 prevented the Park Service from killing burros. We were left with the expensive proposition of capturing and removing the burros. BLM had teams of wranglers which had been removing wild horses from public lands for years. These wranglers were hired by the Park Service.

The wranglers set up their camp across from the ranger station. These wranglers were truly the last of the vintage western cowboy. They loved being cowboys far more than the pay they received and they knew that there were few jobs like this left in the West. They each had a ramada of five to eight horses. Their horses came first and foremost and their tack was the best that could be brought or made. They were bad-ass guys with that true heart of gold that no Hollywood writer could ever recreate.

Our basic operation to capture burros was something out of an action movie. I flew with the contract helicopter, located a group of 20 to 50 burros, then had the wranglers set up below the burros and wait until we drove them with the helicopter down to the wranglers. The wranglers would then either rope the burros or drive them into a portable corral.

In theory it sounded easy, but if we captured a third of the burros we saw, we thought we were doing pretty well. Many times we thought we had the burro captured, then he made some unbelievable move and escaped. I grew to respect the burro as being one smart animal. My respect for the wranglers also grew. Numerous times I saw a horse fall, throwing a wrangler head over heels onto the hard rocky ground. When that happened, we'd circle in the helicopter as the wrangler got up. First he'd check his horse for injuries and then himself. After making sure everything was alright he'd ride back to the corral to pick up another horse and get back in the chase.

I loved the time I spent in the helicopter. Most of the pilots were Viet Nam veterans who loved to fly. There is nothing like skimming across the desert ten feet off the ground going 90 miles an hour making sharp quick turns. Some of the best times were when we had to mark the burros with paintballs. BLM wanted to know if removing burros from one area would then cause burros from another area to move into the newly cleared area. Our job was to mark as many burros as we could in the adjacent areas and then track where they went. For two or three days I sat in the doorway of a Hughes 500 helicopter, my feet on the landing skids shooting a paintball gun at the burros. We had to get within twenty feet of the burro so that the prop wash wouldn't affect the trajectory of the paintball. These were some wild rides and great times.

Wildrose offered a once in a life time experience. To live a life of isolation and total self-reliance is truly unique, but it also takes a toll. Having a small baby and living by ourselves put pressures on Valerie and me. She soon was spending more and more time away from Wildrose. Once during the summer I went sixteen days without talking to anyone. You get to know yourself pretty well. Finally, after twenty-seven months I got a promotion to Callville Bay at Lake Mead National Recreation Area and we moved on to another adventure.

CHAPTER FOUR
FIRST CALL

Lake Mead National Recreation Area, Las Vegas, NV

I was in my patrol car when the call came over the radio that a fight was in progress at the Callville Marina. As the Lake Mead dispatcher got more information, he wanted to get units rolling in that direction. I listened to the other Northshore units call in their locations and I discovered that I was the closest unit. I had only been at Lake Mead for seven days and this was the first time I worked by myself. The other rangers were watching me closely to see what the new guy could do. At that time Lake Mead had the highest graded rangers in the whole Park Service. It was where law enforcement was truly considered important. The rangers that worked there took great pride in their positions and saw themselves as professional law enforcement officers. I had wanted to join this group for a long time and now felt my every move was being studied.

I radioed dispatch that I was en route, turned my patrol car around, hit the siren, and started down the hill towards Callville Bay. As I drove I checked to make sure my baton was handy and went over in my mind what I was doing to do on my arrival. The road to Callville is steep and winding. As I drove into a sharp curve, I saw a late model Cadillac coming towards me. I could tell that the Cadillac was going way too fast for the curve. As I slowed the driver's side wheels came across the double yellow line. I could now see the driver's face as the distance decreased between us. I moved my vehicle completely over to the right shoulder in the dirt, and could go no farther because of a steep cut bank. I looked again at the drivers face and braced for the impact. Just a moment before we were to hit head-on, the driver braked hard causing the Cadillac to go into a four-wheel drift-skid. Instead of hitting head-on the left rear bumper of the Cadillac raked across the left side of my patrol car from the front fender to the rear fender.

As the Cadillac's bumper tore my car, I shot across the lanes and onto the opposite shoulder. I was able to control that skid and stop my vehicle. I looked in my rear view mirror and could see car parts all over the road. I tried to get out of the door, but it was jammed shut. I managed to get my six-foot-six-inch frame over the center console and out the passenger door. Then I saw the driver standing next to his vehicle. I couldn't believe that this had happened to me on my first call! The driver told me he was alright and that the accident was his fault. I radioed the accident report to dispatch and said that I didn't think I could drive my vehicle to the fight call. After I finished the call, the driver sheepishly told me that he was probably the one involved in the fight. He said that he and his girlfriend had been arguing and that he got mad and he drove off in a hurry, leaving her behind.

As the other units arrived, I saw them talking among themselves and thinking that this was not the way to start a new job. After the investigation was complete I was able to limp my patrol car back to Callville Bay. As I got out of my vehicle I saw my wife, Valerie, standing in front of our Park Service trailer with our one-year-old son in her arms. The impact of what had almost happened hit me full force at that moment. As I told her the story I could feel waves of nausea going through my body. I had damned near been killed!

But all I wanted to do now was go out and get back to work. I hugged Valerie and Scott, found another vehicle and went back on patrol.

Justice was served three months later when the Cadillac driver got into another fight with his girl friend. This time I made to the scene on time I arrested the guy and also found cocaine on him.

At my going away party three years later, I found out the story of what the other rangers were all talking about the day of the accident. They had all been glad that I wasn't killed, but they joked what a great story it would have been. In a black humor sort of way it would have made a great story; it was just another example of the macabre ranger sense of humor we all shared.

CHAPTER FIVE
TWO TIMES IN ONE DAY

Lake Mead National Recreation Area, Las Vegas, NV

As Gary and I walked back to the Callville Ranger Station at Lake Mead we talked about how the wind was still coming out of the west, which was unusual for this time of year. The waves on the lake were rolling with about three feet of distance between them with a fine spray blowing off the tops. We both commented on the lone houseboat heading out of the marina. It just didn't seem like a good day to be boating.

Gary and I settled into our desks in the small trailer that served as our ranger station. It had been a busy weekend with lots of reports to write. We had barely started working when the phone rang and the dispatcher said that he had a second hand report that a houseboat was sinking by the entrance buoy to Callville Bay. I grabbed my binoculars and stepped outside the station. Immediately, I saw the same houseboat that left the marina earlier that morning now halfway underwater with its bow rising into the air.

Gary and I ran down the boat ramp and onto the dock and arrived out of breath at the Park Services twenty-four-foot Skipjack boat. We ventilated the engine room, got the twin Volvo engines started and were on our way in less than five minutes. Gary captained the boat as I prepared the throwing lines and life jackets. When Gary and I worked together he always drove the patrol car or the boat.

He was one of those gifted people that had a natural athleticism which allowed his mind and body to work in smooth coordination. At six feet, six inches Gary was as tall as I was, but weighed 100 pounds more, and yet he moved with agility of a much smaller man.

When we arrived at the houseboat, only the front quarter of the boat was above the waterline. The houseboat rose three or four feet each time a wind-driven wave came by. There was a male about thirty-years-old straddling the front railing and we could see two other private boats circling the houseboat. I contacted one of the private boaters on the CB radio who confirmed they'd picked four people out of the water and that there was only one other person on the houseboat.

Gary moved the Skipjack to the leeward side of the houseboat and advanced slowly towards the houseboat so that the starboard side of the Skipjack was perpendicular to the bow of the house-boat. When we had the rear cockpit area of the Skipjack directly in front of the man, I yelled for him to jump onto our boat. As he jumped I grabbed his arm and pulled him into the boat. The force of his jumping and my pulling almost threw him over the port gunwale and into the lake. I held on and he stayed in the boat. He told us his name was Gus and that his brother, Hugo, sister-in-law, Marge, and mother and father had all been rescued by the other two boats and that there was no one else on the houseboat.

Gus explained that the twin outboard engines on the houseboat had both stopped when they were leaving the bay. When he and his brother were working on them, the waves started entering the stern of the houseboat causing it to flood. I put some blankets around Gus and we headed back to the dock.

As we arrive at the boat ramp and could see Gus's brother, Hugo, running towards him. I thought this was going to be a joyful reunion between the two brothers. Instead, Hugo planted a right cross directly to Gus's jaw and the brothers broke into a full out fight. After some effort Gary and I were able to pull the two brothers apart. We didn't understand a thing that was going on because everyone was yelling at each other in Polish. Their mother, wrapped in three blankets, was crying her eyes out and their father had his arms wrapped around his wife while yelling at the top of his lungs. This was not the joyful reunion I was excepting!

Finally Hugo's wife, Marge, stepped forward. She was obviously outraged and disgusted about everything. She explained what was going on. Apparently, this trip had been planned for a long time, and they were determined to go out onto the lake and unfavorable wind and weather wasn't going to stop them. As the houseboat left the marina both engines died and the two brothers went to check out the problem. Since Hugo and Gus both weighed well over 250 pounds each, this put a lot of weight on the back of the boat. Then they were then joined by their mother and father who also weighed at least 250 pounds each. All this weight caused the stern to lower allowing the waves to flood into the boat causing it to sink. As the boat filled with water the mother gripped hold of the inside railing and refused to leave the boat. The water filled the boat until it was up to their chests. The mother still refused to leave and since the father refused to leave without his wife, the situation got desperate. At this point Gus decided he had to do something to get his mother and father out of the boat before it sunk, so he hit her in the jaw and knocked her out. He was then able to get her out of the boat and into a life jacket just as the cabin filled with water. Meanwhile, no one helped Marge get off the boat.

Hugo, Marge said, yelled at Gus since he hit his mother and the father yelled Polish curses at Gus. The two were outraged that Gus hit his mother even though it probably saved her from drowning. Marge truly believed that if Gus hadn't gotten his mother out of the cabin they all would have drowned. She told us that she had had it with this crazy family and planned to go in Vegas and get a divorce. She then walked up to the pay phone and called a taxi.

Since neither of the brothers were seriously hurt, and due to the family dynamics, we decided not to charge either brother with assault. We got all the information we needed and told them they could go home. Hugo got in his car and took his mother and father home. Gus went down to the marina to see about salvaging the boat, and Gary and I returned to the ranger station. About forty-five minutes later we got a call from dispatch that there was a boat sinking in Callville Bay. We told dispatch that this is probably someone reporting the same houseboat. But dispatch said the marina was calling and it's their tow boat that was sinking. Gary and I again launched the Skipjack and headed towards the Callville buoy. We couldn't see anything in the water. As we got closer, we saw Gus and the towboat operator floating in the water. They explained that as soon as they had put a tow line on the bow of the houseboat, it shifted the air pocket causing the houseboat to admittedly sink. They did not have enough time to cut the tow line before the towboat was pulled under along with the houseboat. This had been quite a disastrous day for Gus, sinking two boats and having a huge family blow-up!

CHAPTER SIX
ALEX CHRISTOPHER EWING WAS HERE

Lake Mead National Recreation Area, Las Vegas, NV

Alex Christopher Ewing's first twenty-four years of life had been filled with violence. As a teenager he rolled drunks along the railroad tracks in Kingman, Arizona. He was arrested for burglary and attempted murder after breaking into a couple's home in Kingman and beating the husband with a large rock. As he was transported back to Kingman for trial, he escaped from the Mojave County sheriff's transport van in Henderson, Nevada, just north of Lake Mead National Recreation Area.

The deputies had unchained eleven prisoners so that they could use the bathroom as the deputies refueled the vans. The deputies did a head count as the prisoners returned and discovered that Ewing was missing.

Here's what happened: as soon as the deputies had unchained Ewing, he walked behind the gas station and then ran directly into the neighboring K-Mart and made a beeline for the sporting goods department. There, he exchanged his bright orange jumpsuit for a T-shirt, shorts, and a pair of running shoes. He then ran out of the store and into desert.

In the mid-1980s, Henderson was made up of small blocks of homes separated by large spaces of desert between them. For the next three days Ewing used this design to his advantage. First he broke into several homes to get food and then he found an axe handle. Ewing used the axe handle to break into the home of Chris and Nancy Barry. It was morning and Nancy had just gone down stairs to get some water for her baby when Ewing broke the door window and entered the home. Ewing chased her back upstairs. Chris awoke and just as he rose up on the bed Ewing struck him across the head with the axe handle. The blow was so violent it fractured Chris' skull exposing his brain. Nancy managed to dial 9-1-1 before Ewing turned his attack on her. He broke both her forearms and fractured her wrist as she tried to protect herself. She was finally able to crawl partly under the bed to protect herself and played dead. Ewing stopped beating her. The whole beating was recorded on the 911 tape.

It had was three days since the attack on the Barrys and there had been numerous sightings of Ewing all round Lake Mead, but nothing positive. The general consensus was that Ewing had left the area. Steve, Paul, Dick and I had chased down numerous leads within the recreation area. As we decided what to do for dinner, the phone rang at the Las Vegas Wash Ranger Station. The dispatcher told Steve that Ewing had just made a collect phone call from the Las Vegas Wash Marina to his brother in Kingman. It just seemed like one more wild goose chase, but we got into our patrol cars and drove down to the marina.

Paul and I were in the lead car and Steve and Dick followed. When we approached the ramp leading from the docks, I saw an individual matching Ewing's description walking off the dock. I couldn't believe that it was Ewing and I asked Paul if he thought it was him. Just at that moment Ewing saw us and started running. I gunned the patrol car and braked to a stop just as Ewing jumped from the dock and onto the beach. Paul grabbed the shotgun and I drew my revolver. We both ordered Ewing to stop but he kept running. I ran after him with Paul behind me. The hot humid August air hit my face as I tried to make up ground between Ewing and me. A man launching his small sailboat saw this scene and yelled at me,

"Don't shoot him, he's just a drunk!" I couldn't believe this guy. Here were two rangers chasing a guy with their weapons drawn and all this bystander could do is yell at me.

I was able to keep the same distance between Ewing and I as we ran down the beach, but I wasn't gaining on him. As Ewing ran over a small ridge, Steve broke away to cut him off before he reached the campground. As I ran over the ridge, all I could think of was that Ewing would be waiting for me with a large stick in one hand and a boulder in another. I caught my breath and walked over the ridge which formed a small point out into the lake. At first Ewing was gone, but then I saw him standing at the end of the point with nowhere to go. I aimed my revolver at him and ordered him to raise his hands. He just looked at me. His eyes focused past me and he was balancing on the balls of his feet deciding what to do. I again ordered him to raise his hands and kneel on the ground. Ewing just looked at me. I had a clear shot at him if he ran, but I also didn't see any weapon on him. It would be hard to justify shooting him unarmed. I needed to get closer to Ewing so that I could handcuff him. I raised my voice and again ordered him raise his hands and kneel. As I advanced on Ewing he just stared at me. When I was 10 feet from Ewing he finally raised his hands and went down on the sand. I moved behind him, holstered my weapon, and pinned his right arm to his back with my leg and handcuffed him. Paul caught up. I grabbed Ewing by the hair and yelled at him to never run from me again. This was really a stupid thing to say since I was sure this would never happen again, but the adrenaline of the moment had seized me.

As we walked Ewing back to the patrol car I stopped to tell the bystander who it was we were chasing. The guy just looked at us with disbelief and apologized. By the time we got Ewing back to the ranger station word had gotten out of our capture and the station was full of rangers. The energy in that room was unbelievable; everyone talked at the same time and patted each other on the back. I could barely write my report as we waited for the Henderson Police Department to come and pick up Ewing. The excitement, camaraderie, and energy of the moment burned into my memory. In the years that followed when I got frustrated or upset about what was happening around me, I mentally went back in time to this victorious moment.

Things changed when the Henderson officers arrived. After telling the story of the capture, their immediate response was that I should have shot Ewing. They said that since he was accused of three attempted murders I would have been justified to have shot him. When I reminded them that Ewing wasn't armed they just shook their heads as if I was a fool. I looked at their stomachs hanging over their gun belts and figured the only way they could have caught Ewing was by shooting him. I was surprised that over the next six months every time I booked someone into the Henderson Jail, I was questioned about why I had not shot Ewing.

Ewing was given 110 years in jail for his crimes. Nancy and Chris Barry were unable to live in their house which they considered it a crime scene. They moved and both sustained life-changing injuries. I received over a dozen letters from people thanking me for apprehending Ewing. It certainly felt satisfying to get those letters, but the true hero of the story was the Centel operator who overheard Ewing calling his brother and alerted authorities.

CH🌲PTER SEVEN
RESCUE AT THE MARINA

Lake Mead National Recreation Area, Las Vegas, NV

Dick and I were just leaving the restaurant at Callville Bay when a lady ran up and told us that she could hear cries for help coming from the lake. After calming her down we found out that she had heard a man yelling for help on and off for the last half hour. Dick and I walked out to her houseboat and listened; we couldn't hear anything over the boat traffic leaving the launch ramp. We launched the Skipjack patrol boat and went to investigate.

As we left the marina we heard another boater calling over the CB radio. He had spotted a small outboard boat going in circles just past the Callville entrance buoy and heard someone yelling for help. We arrived at the buoy and I passed my spotlight across it; clinging to the buoy was a man in a swimsuit. We maneuvered over to the buoy and helped him onto our boat.

I smelled the odor of alcohol on his breath; he definitely was intoxicated. He explained that he and a friend had gone into Callville to get some "supplies" and when they were leaving the harbor, the engine died. When he pulled the starter cable on the outboard, the boat had immediately lunged forward and he was thrown off the back of the boat. His friend, Joe, who was at the steering wheel, didn't react. The boat just sailed away. He then swam to the buoy and yelled for help.

We searched for the boat. It didn't take us long to find the boat making large circles just outside the harbor. We saw Joe behind the steering wheel with his head slumped forward, rocking back and forth on his shoulders. We yelled at him, turned on the siren, and flashed our lights, but couldn't get any response out of Joe. It looked as if he were dead.

Now we had a problem. How were we going to stop this boat and board it? After some discussion we decided to throw a towing rope in front of the boat and hope that it got caught in prop. This was easier said than done. After about five tries we gave up on that idea. The next and more dangerous idea was to jump onto the moving boat. Since the boat was going in a circle this wasn't going to be easy.

We decided that Dick would steer the Skipjack and I would jump into the boat. On our first try we just couldn't match the speed of the boats or the angle. Next, we tried a steeper angle. As we approached, a large wave pushed the Skipjack too close to Joe's boat and we crashed hard. The impact caused the windshield to come off Joe's boat hitting him in the chest. Apparently this was just enough of a jolt to wake him up. He grabbed the steering wheel and the boats' paths straighten out. The only problem now was Joe's boat was heading directly towards shore.

We yelled at Joe to stop the boat, but to no avail. We were able to get along side the boat. Dick matched the speed and I jumped into the boat and landed in a pile of beer cans. I put the controls in neutral and stopped the boat. Joe just looked at me with a big drunken smile.

Back at the dock, we pieced their story together. Joe and his friend had been drinking buddies since high school. On this day, they had drunk over two cases of beer and went back to Callville for more. After getting the beer and leaving the marina, the engine died and Joe's friend had gone to the back of the boat to start it. Meanwhile, Joe had left the boat in gear, so as soon as it started, it lunged forward throwing his friend into the water. Joe, thinking everything was alright, just cruised away.

Then he passed out and somehow the steering wheel was thrown hard over causing the boat to go in circles.

I counted over thirty empty cans of beer in the boat along with the two new cases. Joe was arrested for DUI boating and reckless and careless operation. His blood-alcohol level was .201, recorded three hours after the incident; at the time Nevada law stated a blood-alcohol level of .08 was considered intoxicated. Later in Federal court Joe was given a one-year sentence for his offense.

CHAPTER EIGHT
IN THE FACE OF CHANGE

Lassen Volcanic National Park, Mineral, CA

Coming to Lassen Volcanic National Park from Lake Mead I knew there would be change, but I never could image it would be so great.

By this time in my career, I wanted something different, more responsibility, and the chance to use my law enforcement skills. Lassen was an appealing place to work because it was one of the few parks in the United States that had exclusive jurisdiction which meant that only the rangers had authority inside the park. At Lassen, federal laws came before state or county laws and the local sheriffs and highway patrol had no jurisdiction inside the park.

I applied for and got the job as Lassen's primary law enforcement officer, and during the summer months I served as the assistant district ranger for the northern half of the park.

In this position, I quickly learned the difference in attitudes between rangers and upper management after I made my first arrest. I was on patrol when I spotted a car swerving erratically along the park's main road. After a while of working in national parks, I learned the difference between a tourist driving badly and someone who is obviously intoxicated. The driver had the breath of ten thousands beers on him and had another open can of beer between his legs. After giving him a field sobriety test I had no problem arresting him for a DUI. I transported him down to Redding and booked him into the local jail which had a federal contract. I had done this same thing at Lake Mead at least a hundred times.

Then all my problems started. Upset, the park dispatcher called the chief ranger to tell him of the arrest I made. He also called the park superintendent who also got upset that he hadn't been immediately notified.

Their reactions seemed unbelievable to me; I had just taken a dangerous person off the park's road! I soon found out their reason: the district ranger, the chief ranger, and the superintendent had never made an arrest and they were completely amazed that this could happen in their park. They were under the illusion that no crimes happened in the parks and they wanted their records to show exactly that. With an arrest, local papers were bound to pick up on the story and give the park a reputation of an unsafe place to visit. Ultimately, tourism would suffer and upper management would be forced to deal with new challenges. They also were amazed that I would make an arrest without first checking with them. I knew, however, as long as I had followed park service policy and guidelines and worked within the Code of Federal Regulations (CFR) there was nothing wrong with making an arrest. This was my first exposure to the attitudes of this small park where the managers had started their park service careers before law enforcement became an issue and still believed that bad people and things didn't happen in their park.

When I worked at Lassen, it was one of the few parks that had an operating ski lift inside its borders. During the winter Lassen gets an amazing amount of snow, some years as much as 60 feet. Downhill and cross country skiing were major winter activities at the park; people came from throughout the upper Sacramento Valley to ski. I soon learned that other problems were brought into the park. There was open drinking on the ski runs and in the parking lot and by the afternoon I could pick out some pretty intoxicated people. When I asked the district ranger about this, he didn't see any problem and said that I was working at Lassen not Lake Mead and I should stop being such a cop.

Later I found out that the district ranger's way of handling an intoxicated person was to take their car keys away from them and at the end of the day give them back. I asked the district ranger if he gave a field sobriety test to the person before he gave the keys back and he said no. I asked how he knew that the person was sober and could drive and he just looked at me. I checked with the local highway patrol officers and sheriffs deputies and found out they had concerns about the drinking going on in the park. But because they didn't have any jurisdiction in the park they were left with these problems as people left the park.

As the season progressed I started making regular foot patrols of the ski lifts parking lot. I was soon making arrests and giving out citations for underage drinking, public intoxication, and possession of controlled substances. All I basically had to do was walk the lot and I could smell marijuana, see kids snorting cocaine, and catch underage drinkers as they tried to cover up their beer cans in the snow. It was cold hard work, but it was fun and exciting. My main concern was for the safety of the other skiers on the slopes with these impaired people.

I tried to get the district ranger and assistant district ranger involved in these problems. They both felt that there hadn't been a problem before I arrived, so I must be the one causing it. The district ranger finally became so upset with the time I spent on the drug and alcohol problems that he ordered me to spend at least two hours a day skiing the slopes. He couldn't believe that he had to tell a ranger to go skiing. In return, I asked if he would cover the lot when I was on the slopes. His reply was no.

That season there were sixty-nine drug and alcohol related cases. I received no praise or complements for starting to take care of the real problem of visitor safety. I knew in my heart that I was doing the right thing and that public safety was more important than the support of these supervisors.

CH🌲PTER NINE
"BUT WE ARE FROM FRANCE!"

Grand Canyon National Park, Grand Canyon, AZ

National Parks by their very nature draw tourists from all over the world. Grand Canyon being one of the true jewels of the National Park Service was no exception. Of the many different nationalities that I came into contact with, in my experience no group seemed to cause more problems than the French. They were always pushing to the front of a line, irritating other visitors, smoking in no smoking areas, and—one of my favorites—parking their rental cars in places that no one had thought of or tried before, such as directly in front of the doors of the visitor center. Naturally when they did that, I had to write a citation and tow their vehicle. Invariably, the excuse was, "But we are from France!" which I truly believe they thought gave them carte blanche throughout the world.

On a rainy monsoon-driven day in August, I got a call from one of my rangers that a rental car was parked in the fire lane at the Bright Angel Lodge. The Bright Angel is a beautiful old wooden lodge perched on the edge of the canyon. It was very important to keep the fire lanes open in case a fire or medical emergency. Because of the many problems we had towing rental cars the ranger wanted to make sure that I approved the towing. The vehicle not only blocked the fire lane, but partially blocked the regular road I approved the tow.

About two hours later the towing company called to say that there was an irate person at the garage who refused to pay a tow bill. As soon as I arrived I heard the rapid broken English of a Frenchman named Pepé. Pepé stood about six feet tall and was dressed in a multi-colored tank top of which none of the colors could be found in nature. Blue Speedo swimming trunks and sandals completed his wardrobe.

The manager of the garage explained that Pepé refused to pay the towing charge and he had threatened the manager. He then introduced me to Pepé and explained that I was the supervisor who had approved the tow.

Pepé said, "You look like a man of knowledge and understanding." He went on to tell me his story. He and his wife had found a purse while they were walking along the rim. They had left their parking space at the Bright Angel and drove over to the Visitor Center to turn in the purse. The monsoon rains had started while they were gone and when they returned to the parking lot, there were no spaces left to park. Instead of parking in the street they parked in the fire lane because they didn't want to get wet after returning from their good deed. Pepé stated that since he had done this good deed he should be excused from where he had parked. To him it was just a matter of simple logic, his good deed allowed him to break the law.

I thanked Pepé for turning in the purse and told him it was the right thing to do. I said I was sorry that it was raining when he returned and that there were no parking spaces. I also told him that by parking where he had, he had endangered the safety of many people and that one good deed does not allow you to commit a bad deed. Pepé's faced dropped at my response. He said that I looked like an educated man and he would explain it to me again. I repeated my response. At that moment he took a step back and extended his right arm to its full length and with the back of his hand he waved at me and said, "You may go now, you are nothing but an uneducated Reagan Cowboy."

I have to say, this had taken me aback for a second, but I had to smile. I was dealing with someone from France and I knew they always had some type of excuse for their actions. Pepé was just little more creative.

I informed Pepé that I may well be a "Reagan Cowboy," but if he didn't pay the tow bill he wasn't going to get his car back and I was sure the rental company would charge him a lot if he didn't return their vehicle. I also told him that I was going to make sure and follow up to see that he paid his citation for illegal parking. If he didn't pay before he left the United States I'd be sure a US Marshal would be waiting for him as he tried to leave the country. Pepé just turned his back on me.

The next day Pepé returned and paid the towing and impound charge. I checked on his citation about two weeks later and found that he had paid it. I guess there is justice sometimes, but just not the way Pepé viewed it.

CH🌲PTER TEN
ILLEGAL BEAD SELLERS

Grand Canyon National Park, Grand Canyon, AZ

When I arrived at Grand Canyon National Park, the Park Service had finally been given a small amount of extra money to combat the problem of "bead selling." Bead sellers were mostly Navajos Indians who illegally set up selling operations at various overlooks in the park. They sold cheap earrings and necklaces made of wire and colored beads. They attached the jewelry to large bed sheets so they could be rolled up quickly when rangers were spotted in the area. At first glance, the selling of Native American handiwork seemed relatively harmless outside the fact that the Park Service has specific laws against such operations.

The real problem was that at times whole clans of Navajos would take over a vista point, blocking all access. There also were fights between different clans for the right to sell at some of the more popular vista points. Secondary crimes were also committed as visitors left their vehicles unattended and sellers would steal their valuables.

Another problem was sales intimidation. One afternoon while working undercover I watched a group of elderly Italian tourists look at some jewelry and then walk away without buying anything. A large Navajo man then walked over to one of the elderly Italian men, about 80-years-old, and escorted him back to one of the sheets covered with beads. I saw the Navajo point out some jewelry that the man then bought. I followed their tour bus out to their next stop. I contacted the elderly man. In broken English he told me that the "friendly Indian" had said he needed to buy something before he looked at the canyon. The Italian said he understood what was going on and felt that he had little choice but to buy something. He kind of smiled at me like he had done the right thing. He thought that in America this type intimidation was accepted. He was surprised when I apologized for what had happened to him and promised to try and do some about it.

The Navajos had developed an intricate system of counter surveillance to stop us from arresting them. They posted numerous look-outs on the roads leading into the vista points. The lookouts had CB radios or small handsets and they could call in the arrival of law enforcement vehicle before we could witness the actual selling taking place. As we increased pressure on the sellers, their method of selling changed. They knew we didn't want to arrest any children, so we saw children selling the beads and then passing the money to their parents who sat in a truck watching.

We increased our undercover operations by engaging as many different law enforcement rangers as possible. Sometimes we used young, seasonal rangers who went under cover as newlyweds on a honeymoon. They would ooh and ah at the jewelry, take pictures of each other and most importantly, get the bead seller in the picture along with the price attached jewelry. One ranger would then step aside and call on the radio advising us they had enough probable cause to make an arrest. We usually knew where the lookouts were stationed and how long it would take to get to the vista point after the law enforcement vehicle was spotted. We timed our arrival just as the arrest was being made. Oftentimes the bead sellers resisted arrest and we didn't want the undercovers left too long without back up. As a side note, many of these young couple teams not only made some good arrests, they also started some interesting romances, one of which lead to a marriage.

During the winter I worked as the night shift supervisor starting at 5:00 p.m. Sometimes I took my son, Scott, out for a drive before the shift started. We would visit the various points and would run into bead sellers. Scott always liked to listen to my law enforcement stories, so he knew about the bead sellers and how we worked them. Scott became a natural at working the sellers. He would pick up a piece of jewelry and show it to me and say how much his mother would love that piece. He'd ask if we could buy it and then I said yes. He would then ask the price and I would usually take a picture of him with the jewelry. He would make the whole case without me saying a thing. I would then take him home and at the start my shift arrange for the arrest of the bead sellers. This was a great father-son bonding experience.

After a year we started to put a dent in the bead sellers operations in the park. Some tourists missed the sellers, but most of the returning tourists commented on how much nicer it was without them.

CH🌲PTER ELEVEN
UNFORGETTABLE DAYS AT THE GRAND CANYON

Grand Canyon National Park, Grand Canyon, AZ

The best job I ever had during my thirty years as a ranger was the five years I spent as a shift supervisor on the South Rim of the Grand Canyon. I loved the beauty and changing moods of the canyon and I loved the action. Lake Mead came close, but nothing topped the Canyon for the diversity of experiences from structural and wildland fires, to major medical and law enforcement incidents.

As shift supervisor I directed the responses for all of these incidents twelve hours a day and when off duty, I was on call to support the other rangers. Along with supervising the eight rangers on my shift I was also qualified as an emergency medical technician, structural fire truck engineer and fire captain. I also served as a member of the search and rescue team and held numerous wildland fire fighting qualifications. Those five years were an adrenaline junkie's dream. Although, in one particular ten-day period, even I thought things were getting a little intense.

It started with the arrest of J.D. Green, a concession employee who was found with five pipe bombs and a half pound of plastic explosives in his car. Green had been working in the area for about three months. He had a shaved head and wore military clothing. I had stopped him twice for minor traffic violations and once saw him trying to translate a Russian weapons manual one word at a time at the Bright Angel Bar. The Coconino County deputy sheriffs and all the rangers had been keeping an eye on him, but he had never done anything wrong until one night there was a loud explosion in the forest.

The next day Green bragged to some of his fellow employees about the bomb he had made. He even went so far as to show one of the employees a pipe bomb. This was enough information for us to find Green and search his car. We found a loaded AK-47 assault rifle and 1500 rounds of ammunition, plastic explosives, and five pipe bombs. When questioned, Green stated that his goal was to blow a hole in the park entrance road and shut down the park. This was almost twelve years before 9/11.

A few days later I received a call that a ten-year-old boy had collapsed at the backcountry office. Upon arrival I found Patrick Kelly lying on the floor. Kelly was not breathing, but his heart was still beating. As Kelly's mother pleaded for him to start breathing, the other rangers, Sherrie, Bev, and Nancy, tried everything they knew to revive him. They established an airway and gave him oxygen. We transported him to the clinic and then had a Life Flight helicopter transport him to Flagstaff where the doctors declared him brain-dead. Apparently he had suffered a brain aneurysm. The mother's anguish and pain hit me hard; my son, Scott, was the same age and I knew how I'd feel if the same thing had happened to me.

The following morning, Roy Deavon died of a heart attack at Yavapai Point. Deavon was in his sixties and visiting from England. This was his first time to the Grand Canyon and he wanted to witness it with a sunrise. He had been sitting on a rock and had just fallen over as the first sun rays hit the canyon walls. By the time we got to him he had been without oxygen for over forty-five minutes. His pupils were dilated and there was no pulse or breathing sounds. He was declared dead at the scene.

Next came the first thunderstorms of the monsoon season which ignited numerous fires along the North Rim of the canyon. I worked on a crew setting a backfire to block the advance of a large fire. We lit off the fire and then a thunderstorm came over the burning area. Lighting fell all around us. The wind blew hard and a heavy rain poured down; all of nature's furry was happening at the same time.

While conducting flights along the canyon rim looking for other fires, the helicopter crew found what appeared to be a body about 400 feet below the El Tovar Hotel. We sent a crew down on ropes to investigate. They discovered the headless corpse of a man. The skin was dried to the bones indicting that he had been there for a while. We didn't have any reports of missing persons, and for the rest of my time at Grand Canyon we never discovered his identity.

Two nights later I got a call from dispatch that Brian, the night shift supervisor, requested assistance for a rollover vehicle accident on the dump road south of the park. A group of former Grand Canyon High School students had been partying in the forest. On the way back to the park the driver had rolled his CJ-5 Jeep. All the occupants were ejected.

When I arrived Brian was administering CPR on a female and waved for me to come over and help him. I could see that her skull was deformed and glistening white in the moonlight. She was completely scalped by the impact. As I knelt down to help Brian, I felt a wetness on my knee. I had accidentally put my knee onto some of her brain tissue which had leaked out of her skull. We worked on her for fifteen minutes before the Flagstaff medical staff declared her deceased. I next went over to the driver who didn't appear to be seriously injured. I asked him what his problem was and he stated that he was holding his whole face on. As he removed his hand all the skin from hairline to his eye brows fell forward. I wrapped his forehead in bandages then transported him to the clinic.

The final incident happened when Benjamin Rieder rode his bike back to Victor Hall from Tusayan after working at the new McDonald's. Rieder was a nice guy that worked for the Fred Harvey Concession. He was a hard worker that wanted to make some extra money. He had finished his night shift and was riding his bike, without any lights, along the park road when he was struck by a Jeep. Rieder was thrown about 60 feet and landed in the dirt shoulder off the road. The impact broke both his legs above and below his knees and both his arms, he also suffered major internal injuries. I had never seen a body so deformed. We stabilized the injuries as best we could and transported him to the clinic. The Life Flight helicopter arrived just as we got to the clinic, so we immediately placed him in the helicopter. As we lifted him in, his blood ran off the plastic stretcher and onto us. He literally had so many holes in him he was bleeding out all his blood. Rieder died in the helicopter.

Things slowed down for a while after that incident, but at Grand Canyon it never really stopped; there was always something happening to keep a ranger busy.

CH🌲PTER TWELVE
THE LAST PEOPLE TO SEE IT

Yellowstone National Park, WY

The fires in Yellowstone National Park had been burning since early July and had grown to nearly a million acres in size by the time I arrived at the Clover-Mist Fire. For the past decade the winter snowpack had been below normal, but the summers had been cool and moist. The summer of 1988 started much the same way as past summers, and the fire managers allowed natural lightening-caused fires to burn without suppression, hoping for summer rains to contain the fires. But almost no precipitation fell in July and August for the first time in the 112 years of weather observations. With high daytime temperatures, low humidity, and strong gusty winds, fire conditions changed rapidly and soon the fires were out of control.

I knew this was something big and I wanted to be part of it. I still held a Red Card from my seasonal days at Glacier National Park, and was qualified for many different firefighting jobs.

I was a little disappointed when I arrived at the Jackson Hole airport and was assigned to the Corral Fire on the Bridger National Forest 90 miles south of Jackson Hole. The Corral Fire had just started and they needed firefighters immediately so those of us who were standing in line to check in at that moment were just given maps and the keys to trucks and told to drive to the fire.

I arrived at the fire camp at one o'clock in the morning. The camp was completely surrounded by fire. All night long as I tried to sleep I could see and hear trees burning and falling.

Later I was assigned to the Plans Section as a field observer. This job mainly consisted of scouting the fire line and making fire weather reports. Even with all the modern fire technology you still need a person on the ground mapping and reporting back current fire conditions. Since there weren't enough firefighters, my job quickly turned into a one-man fire attack team. I would find spot fires forming in front of the fire and either build a fire line around it or get the one helicopter we had to make a water drop of it. This went on for five days until more crews could be brought into the area. The eighteen-hour days were exhausting, but the sense of satisfaction at the end of day was exhilarating. The fire spread was reduced and with the extra crews finally contained to 4200 acres.

I got one night of rest in Jackson Hole and was transported over to West Yellowstone. The afternoon I arrived, the North Fork Fire was making a run towards the town. As the sun set the light shown a golden white against the gigantic smoke column raising 20,000 feet into sky. The fire was about five miles from the town but the wind gusts were traveling 20 to 30 miles per hour as the air was being pulled towards the fire. There was a sense that nature was in total control and we were just sitting on the edge waiting for her next move.

The next morning I drove over to Camp Crandall — the incident camp for the Clover-Mist Fire. The Clover and Mist Fires had joined together on July 22 to form a large, complex fire which burned outside Yellowstone National Park and onto the Crandall District of the Shoshone National Forest.

The camp was situated on a small knoll above the Crandall Ranger Station. The area normally served as a garbage transfer point and that set the tone for the camp. The camp looked like some of the pictures I'd seen of the early Gold Rush towns in the hills of California. It had two streets at right angles to each other with plywood shacks lining each side. The shacks housed the various camp functions: security, finance, laundry, first aid, the commissary, telephones and satellite television. At the street intersection was a huge circus-like tent which housed the mess hall. Outside the mess tent there was a series of heating units called salamanders. These salamanders looked and acted like the smudge pots used to keep the air moving in orchards. People always stood around them to keep warm and bullshit with each other. To finally top off the scene, the streets were constantly being wet down to keep the dust under control. As the nights got colder, the streets froze. During the height of the fire there were over two-thousand people living at Camp Crandall.

The first night there, I slept in a tent with twelve other people. I didn't get much sleep with everyone coughing, farting, snoring and getting up to go to the bathroom. The next day I found a tarp and made a small lean-to and slept under it for the rest of my stay. Another thing that made life at Crandall interesting was trying to find a portable toilet which wasn't filled to the seat. Crandall was a remote location and the portable toilets weren't pumped out as often as they should have been. Most mornings I had to walk around until I found a toilet that I could rock back and forth to even out the load a little and then took my chances with the splash zone.

When the plans chief found out that I knew how to ride a horse, I was assigned to mapping the fire advance along the Tepee, Tough, and Squaw Creek drainages. The smoke was so dense that we couldn't see anything from the air and the infra-red photos only give a general view. The job required riding a horse approximately 9 miles up the North Fork of Crandall Creek and then mapping the fires location and taking hourly weather observations.

I was given a guide since I didn't know the area. His name was Brad and his father had been the Forest Service District Ranger for this area. Brad had grown up in the Shoshone National Forest and knew it like the back of his hand. Brad looked and acted like a true cowboy. He was the real deal, from his manner to the expert way he kept and handled his equipment and animals. The first day he put all sorts of little tests in front of me like everyone does who knows their job, but isn't sure about the new guy. I guess I passed most of them because I quickly gained his confidence.

I think Brad knew that there was no stopping this fire until the snows arrived. When he found out I was as interested in the outdoors as he was, he started showing me his favorite places. One morning he had me arrive before dawn and we reached the end of the drainage just as the sun was rising. We got off our horses and walked up to a little saddle back between two rock ridges. Brad pointed to one of the old blown-over trees and there, in the rising sunlight, was the biggest mule deer I had ever seen. The deer just walked along the ridgeline and then dropped into the drainage. Brad told me that he had been watching that mule deer for the last three years. He knew he could have made a lot of money guiding someone to that deer, but it was just too beautiful of an animal to kill. During the next days between mapping and weather observations, Brad showed me his hunting camps, grizzly dens, hidden pools with large trout, and the bones of a horse he had shot and used as bait for hunting bears.

Meanwhile, the fire just kept growing bigger each day we rode up the drainage. Based on my reports and other observations, the fire operations chief decided that the only way to stop this branch of the fire was to build a dozer line. This drainage and ridgelines were all within a wilderness area which excluded the use of dozers for fire fighting, so this decision had not been made easily. The damage to the area increased and Brad and I knew the end was near for his beloved area. The next day Brad hardly spoke a word as we rode up the trail. After I took my weather observations and completed mapping the fire front, Brad and I sat in the sun and watched hawks dive on small mice and voles as the ran away from the fire. Brad told me story after story of his years growing up in this drainage, it was a complete outpour of one man's love and relationship with a place. The ride back to camp was done in silence.

The next day the dozers started up the drainage and the fire grew larger. Brad didn't show up for work that day and I never saw him again. I was glad that I was with him during the last days that the forest had existed as he had known it all those years.

Since I was the only one that knew the area, I ended up being in charge of the dozer crews as they tried to make a fire line to stop the blaze. But each day the winds kept blowing and on the third day a major effort was mounted to contain the fire before it made a run towards Crandall. Three large Chinook helicopters ferried in 125 firefighters to the ridge. I rode with two crews inside one of the Chinooks. Most of the crew members were from the San Carlos Apache Tribe and had never flown in a helicopter. There were a lot of wide-eyed firefighters by the time the helicopter made a two-point landing on the side of the ridge.

All day the crews and dozers worked together to build the line, but as the afternoon winds grew and the relative humidity dropped lower, the fire grew and broke over the line. Just as the sun was setting, I was told that there were three slurry bombers available to make fire retardant drops. I made contact with the spotter plane and it turned out to be someone I had worked with at Lassen Volcanic National Park. After a quick conversation we lined up where the drops would be placed. The pilot made two quick passes to make sure there were no down drafts and then lead the bombers into the fire. It was truly a beautiful sight to see the bright red slurry fall from the bomb bay doors all lit up in the evening sunlight.

Again the winds and the intensity of the fire were too strong and the fire continued its race forward. Because of the latest of the slurry drops, not all the crews were able to be airlifted off the ridge. I knew the way out and volunteered to lead the remaining two crews the eight miles back to the pickup point. It was a long hike after a long day. We made it back to camp at 11:30 p.m. The next day it was decided to give up trying to stop the fire in the upper drainage and concentrate on the valley. There were numerous vacation homes and lodges in the area around the Crandall Ranger Station and the objective shifted to protect these structures. Since I was qualified with the Park Service as both a structural fire captain and engineer, I was assigned to protect the K Bar Z Ranch by Swamp Lake. The idea was to build a dozer line in back of the ranch from Oliver Gulch to Swamp Lake and then foam the ranch buildings protect them.

The fire was now a raging engine pushed down the drainage by its own force. The sky was blotted out by smoke and flames which rose hundreds of feet above the trees. The only sound was the roar of the flames.

The line was barely built before the fire sped up to it. I was working with a small 500-gallon pumper and three 1,000-gallon pumpers that had been brought all the way from Kansas.

The crews were made up of farmers who normally worked as volunteers. They were used to fighting grass fires and had never faced anything like this. I had them lay outlines all around the building and we had fixed nozzles to constantly spray water on the main structures. The fire moved to within 75 feet of the buildings. The roar was now like a jet engine with the wind being pulled towards the fire. At times the flames reached over us, but we continued to put out spot fires ignited from the falling embers. For three hours we never stopped moving. We were able to save the ranch buildings, but there was nothing left standing around it. Now there were only buildings surrounded by white ash with small thin sticks standing where several 150-feet lodge-pole trees once stood.

The owner returned later that night and shook all our hands and thanked us with tears running down his face. I felt we didn't deserve his thanks, as all he had were these buildings in a sea of smoldering ash.

I stayed on doing various jobs for the next week and then was demobilized back to Grand Canyon after serving my twenty-five days. The Yellowstone Fires were not extinguished until December when the heavy snows returned to the park. When Nature takes control there's no stopping her.

CH🌲PTER THIRTEEN
"KNIVES WERE INVOLVED"

Grand Canyon National Park, Grand Canyon, AZ

The call came in from dispatch that there was a fight in progress at Victor Hall. Dispatch also said that knives were involved. I had just finished dinner at my house on Apache Way and Laura just finished up on a call at the Muswik Lodge; we both arrived at Victor Hall in about two minutes. Victor Hall was used as concession employee housing; sometimes we called it "Victim Hall." Since Laura and I were the only ones on shift that night, we decided to split up and enter the hall from different directions. We agreed that once we made it up to the second floor she would cover me with her Remington 870 shotgun while I searched the hallway to find out what had happened.

As I started down the hallway, the place looked like a game my son played at Chucky Cheese. Heads were popping in and out of doorways and people ran from room to room. Confusion was a main component. I drew my Smith & Wesson Model 19 revolver and started down the hallway.

As I passed each open door I checked inside to make sure that it was clear and safe before continuing forward. The last thing I wanted was to have someone come out of a room after I had checked it with a knife or something worst. Halfway down the hall a man stood just inside an open doorway. There was blood on his T-shirt and his left eye was swollen. I recognized him as Jim, one of the cooks from the El Tovar Hotel. Jim had a long history of drug and alcohol problems and I had arrested him before.

When he saw me, Jim immediately stepped farther back into his room. At first both hands were in front of him, then a moment later, he jerked his right hand behind his back and kept it there. Jim seemed dazed and confused. I ordered him to show me his right hand, but he just stared at me. I brought my revolver up to eye level and aligned my sights on his chest. I again ordered him to show me his hand. I could feel the world slow down like it always does for me at moments like these. The adrenaline surges through the body and everything becomes sharper, clearer and more focused. I knew that if he held a knife I would have little time to react. Automatically my mind checked off all the things I needed to do before Jim's next move.

There was a solid background of concrete blocks behind him which meant if I missed my shot, the bullet wouldn't strike anything else. I knew that for my own morality and conscious, I had to see a weapon and feel the threat before I could pull the trigger. I yelled at Jim again to bring his hand out slowly. On my own gun, I could see the hammer move toward me as I put more pressure on the trigger. I was mentally prepared for Jims' next move.

Jim slowly took his right hand out from behind his back. There was nothing in his hand. I took the pressure off the trigger and the hammer moved slowly away from me gently resting against the cylinder.

I holstered my revolver, stepped forward, and grabbed Jim by his left arm and pushed him against the wall. I lifted up his T-shirt and there in the small of his back was a 12-inch Marine Corp K-Bar fighting knife. I removed the knife and placed it in the back of my equipment belt. I shouted to Laura to cover me as I backed Jim down the hall and out of the building.

By this time dispatch called other off-duty rangers to the scene and we were able to piece the story together of what had happened. Apparently Jim had been making some bad drug deals at Victor Hall. This caused hard feelings that had come to a head when Jim returned to Victor Hall that evening. There was a fight and Jim had drawn his knife. When I questioned Jim about why he had gone and reached behind his back after he had seen me he said,

"I just wanted to show you the knife." I told him that could have been a fatal mistake that I had no way of knowing that the knife wouldn't have been used on me. He then said he had thought about it for a second and had decided that if he had brought the knife out, he was pretty sure I would have shot him. He didn't think that would have been such a good thing for either of us. The way he said this made me believe that he had given some thought to using that knife on me.

After hearing Jim's story I was so glad for my training and that rush of adrenaline. They both worked together to get me through this incident without having to kill someone. The other great thing was that later that evening, Laura came up to me and told me that for the first time in her career she knew that someone was depending on her to protect them. Laura said she was watching over me and knew that if she had to pull the trigger she would not have hesitated.

CH🌲PTER FOURTEEN
TOO MUCH FOR ONE DAY

California Desert District, Palm Springs, CA

As I drove under the railroad trestle at Salt Creek and up Gucci Wash my mind was a long way from expecting to run into nine Asian and Arab men wearing camouflage clothes and shooting assault weapons. But there they were, standing in a crowd, in front of me I got out of my patrol vehicle and ordered the men to put down their weapons and sit by the campfire. As they complied, I informed them that I needed to check their weapons to see if they were in violation of state or federal weapons laws. They all seemed to understand and appeared to be cooperative. Of the twelve weapons I looked at, five were illegal. I also ran into a terrified pit bull dog hiding under one of the pick-up trucks. I always liked it when the dog was more scared of me then I was of it.

I tried to call in my contact to dispatch, but only got static. After twelve years of complaining about the radio system and management lack of response, I wasn't surprised or worried. When you're a ranger you accept and train to handle any situation by yourself.

After I found out who the weapons belonged to, I started writing citations. I had written the second citation when the Arab gentlemen named Akbar stepped forward and informed me that everyone there was an outstanding citizen and really good guy. He also said that he worked for the FBI and he thought I should give them a break. I asked if he was an agent and why he hadn't identified himself earlier. He again said he worked for the FBI. When I asked him for some FBI identification he could only show me his driver's license. I asked him to step back by the campfire while I completed writing the rest of the citations. By this time, it was after sunset and even though everything was going well, I didn't want to be there any longer than I needed to be with that many armed individuals. I cleared the area and drove east on Bradshaw Trail.

As I got into a better radio communication area I heard Fred calling my radio number. He had heard me trying to call dispatch and was coming to back me up. I told him I was alright and we agreed to meet at Gasline Road and Bradshaw Trail. We had earlier planned to do a nighttime surveillance for illegal alien smugglers crossing onto Bureau of Land Management lands from the Chocolate Mountain Bombing Range. When I arrived, Fred was parked by the northwest corner of the intersection about 200 meters onto the desert pavement. This was a favorite location of ours because we could watch the intersection and not be seen. Like anyone who has just had an adventure I had to tell my story of the assault weapons and the Arab guy who claimed to work for the FBI.

I barely completed my story before we heard the unmistakable rattle of a vehicle driving north from the bombing range. There were no headlights visible so I reached for my night vision goggles and watched as a Jeep Cherokee sped north on Gasline Road towards the I-10 Freeway 11 miles away. Since it's illegal to trespass on the bombing range we had probable cause to stop the vehicle. In all likelihood this vehicle was smuggling human beings.

Fred was already ahead of me and after the vehicle. His vehicle had been "lifted" and outfitted with a heavier suspension and bigger tires so he could go faster than me. After about a mile Fred caught up to the Jeep and activated his overhead lights. The driver just sped up. Fred continued after the Jeep and I contacted dispatch and had them notify Border Patrol and the Highway Patrol that we had a smuggling vehicle en route to the Red Cloud on-ramp for the I-10 Freeway.

Fred suddenly came back on the radio and informed me that the driver of the Jeep tried to run him off the road. Along with the trespassing and smuggling charges, the driver added assault on a federal officer to his bulging violation count. The chase continued towards the I-10. As we approached the Red Cloud on-ramp, Fred and I decided that it would be too dangerous to continue the chase onto the freeway, but we thought we might be able to stop it before it got to the interstate.

As the road got wider near the on-ramp Fred accelerated his vehicle around the Jeep causing it to turn right towards the eastbound entrance to the freeway. I was now behind the Jeep. As we drove east a highway patrol vehicle suddenly turned on its headlights and overhead lights blinding the driver and causing the Jeep to miss the freeway entrance.

We drove cross-country heading eastbound parallel to the freeway. I suddenly came to a stop as my patrol vehicle dropped into a two-foot-deep ravine. Fred continued the chase as I tried to get out of the ravine. Fred and I had decided that when the chase ended, our main concern would be getting the driver and not worrying about the rest of the illegal aliens.

I got unstuck and saw a cloud of dust in my headlights and knew the chase was over. The Jeep dropped into a deeper ravine than the one I had run into. Fred yelled that the driver was wearing black and he was in foot pursuit. I could see numerous people running and the man in black tried to get under the highway fence. Fred did the same thing. I tried to go through the fence, but my jacket got caught on the barbed wire.

I finally got free and saw two highway patrol officers' guns drawn with two subjects on the ground. One was our man in black. I went forward and handcuffed him and Fred handcuffed the other. We knew there were at least eight other subjects at large. The man in black spoke good English at first, but as I asked the question who was driving, he suddenly lost his ability to speak or understand English. I did find a wallet with driver's license, money, and a cell phone which all pointed to the fact that he was the driver and smuggler.

A short time later Border Patrol arrived and we found six other illegal aliens none of whom carried any money or identification. One had a swollen left arm which he probably broke while the driver tried to evade us. An inspection of Fred's vehicle showed that the rear shocks were broken. I transferred the man in black to my vehicle, had Fred's vehicle towed and then drove to the Blythe Jail to book the subject. The next day the district attorney charged the man in black with two counts of felony assault on a police officer, the second charge was filed because Fred's police dog, Scout, was considered a fully certificated police officer. The Border Patrol ran a fingerprint check on the man in black and found that he had been caught before for illegal alien trafficking. So he was given an automatic year in jail.

The next day Fred, Javier, and I went back to Gucci Wash to figure out the story of the FBI employee. We arrived just as the group was breaking camp. I asked to speak to Akbar. His friends said he was off hiking. We waited over an hour when suddenly we heard rocks falling from a cliff above.

There was Akbar climbing down the rock face carrying a Remington Model 700 bull barrel rifle with a sniper scope attached, wrapped in desert camouflage. When he arrived, I asked him what he had been doing and he stated he had been watching us. Nothing makes the hair on the back of your neck stand up faster than the knowledge that someone has been looking at you though the crosshairs of a rifle.

I told Akbar that I was concerned that he had may have falsely identified himself as an FBI employee. Akbar then stated that he was an informant for the FBI and was going to Iraq in the next month and gave me his agents name and telephone number. I was able to contact the agent who confirmed Akbar's identity. The agent had many concerns about my contacts with Akbar, especially about his coming forward and saying he worked for the FBI. Two days later I received a request for a copy of my report and was told that Akbar would not be working with the FBI anymore.

CH🌲PTER FIFTEEN
EXTRA SUPPORT

California Desert District, Palm Springs, CA

I had just turned south into Salt Creek Valley from the Summit Road, when I heard the rifle fire. Hundreds of shots fired in quick succession; I got out my spotting scope and scanned the surrounding hills. I couldn't see anything so I moved slowly down the valley. I drove about a mile west when I caught the reflection of a windshield. Through my scope I saw numerous vehicles and a large American flag blowing in the wind.

The firing stopped as I got out of my patrol vehicle and started walking up the ridgeline towards the vehicles. I got to a location where I could look down into the camp. There were eight vehicles parked in a semicircle with two olive drab tents. The most disturbing thing I saw were the numerous gun cases laying on the ground and a freshly dug defensive trench which faced towards the valley.

I radioed my location to dispatch and requested back-up. Everyone was at least an hour away. As I scanned the surrounding hills I saw two males dressed in camouflage, walking downhill towards the camp. Both carried assault rifles and sidearms. I moved to a concealed location and waited. Suddenly one individual appeared in front of me. He was no longer carrying a rifle, but had an automatic pistol. I stepped forward and asked him what was going on. He became extremely irate and barked that he didn't have to tell me anything. At this moment I saw a tall male walking down the next wash. It appeared that he was trying to get around me. I could see that he was wearing an assault vest and carried an AR-15 assault rifle. Feeling that things were escalating quickly, I reached forward and was able to remove the sidearm from the male I was standing next to. I ordered him back to his camp and went looking for the tall male.

As I came over a small ridge, I saw the tall male who was now dressed only in camouflage and no longer wore the assault vest, nor was he carrying the assault rifle. He was in a crouched position walking towards the camp. I ordered him to halt and he raised his hands. I had him turn around, pulled up his shirt and lifted his pant legs so I could see if he had any weapons on him. I then moved forward, patted him down, and found that he wasn't carrying anything. I asked him where the assault rifle was and he just looked at me. I told him that I had seen him wearing the assault vest and carrying the rifle. He then said that he was scared and didn't know if it was legal for him to have the rifle. He said when he saw me talking to his friend he hid the vest and rifle under a creosote bush. I followed his footprints and found the rifle and vest. I picked them up and walked back to the camp.

At this point I saw an airplane flying down the valley; it was H-63, the California Highway Patrol Cessna 187. Then I heard Mike, the patrol pilot, calling over the radio. Mike had been patrolling the I-10 corridor 12 miles away and heard that I was in contact with armed subjects. He came to back me up. The California Highway Patrol air operations were always monitoring our radio frequency because they knew we were usually hours away from back up. As Mike circled the area, I questioned the two males. They finally told me that they were a group of friends that came out to the desert to practice military tactics and that there were eight other individuals out patrolling west of my location. I radioed this information to Mike and he started making low passes over the valley. After about fifteen minutes he located the group lying in a small ravine about a quarter-mile from my location. They were laid out in squad formation with weapons pointing in my direction. After numerous passes with the plane he was able to get them to raise their weapons and walk towards me. As they approached my location, two F-16 Navy fighter jets came off the Chocolate Mountain Bombing Range and flew down the valley a close 500 feet off the ground. They flew on either side of Mike's plane and were gone in a second. Mike later said he didn't see them coming and only saw the shadow of one of the planes after the fact.

There I was with eight individuals all dressed in full military camouflage and carrying a full assortment of weapons, AR-15's, shotguns, and a Remington 700 sniper rifle. As each individual approached me, I had them lay their weapons down and sit down back in camp. One of them made the comment that I must be a pretty important dude to get a spotter plane and two F-16s to cover me. I just smiled and said that being a law enforcement officer is like belonging to the world's largest gang, we all support each other.

A little while later Don and Ronnie arrived and we were able to determine what was going on. This was a small paramilitary group out of Los Angeles who came out to the desert to practice tactics. This in itself was not illegal, but the fact that six of the weapons were not registered, and one of the weapons looked to have been fully automatic, these were the problems for which I issued citations and these were the reasons I turned the weapons in for evidence and turned over the information to the Bureau of Alcohol, Tobacco and Firearms.

CH🌲PTER SIXTEEN
ONE LUCKY MAN

California Desert District, Palm Springs, CA

I t was another hot August day as I drove west on the Coachella Canal. I hadn't seen anyone all day long and was looking forward to going home, jumping into the pool, and cooling off. Just then something caught my eye. I saw two new Ford pick-up trucks with their doors open and no one around them.

I got out of my patrol vehicle and looked inside the trucks. On the seats were gun cases and plastic bags which contained boxes of ammunition. I heard voices coming from a small wash just behind the trucks. I tried to call in my location to dispatch, but as usual there was no response.

As I walked towards the wash I saw three adult men and three small boys. Three rifles laid against the cliff wall and that one of the adults was wearing a sidearm. The rifles appeared to be assault rifles.

I shouted hello to them and climbed down into the wash. I asked if they had been shooting and explained to them that it was illegal to shoot at glass bottles in Riverside County. I then said that I needed to check the rifles to see if they qualified as assault weapons under the California State weapons code.

As I turned towards the rifles the man with the sidearm, who I later found out was named George, took the pistol out of its holster and started raising it towards me. At this moment everything in my mind stopped running at normal speed and went into slow motion. The pistol was now about at my thigh level, and moving towards my stomach. My right hand reached for my Sig Sauer 40 cal. pistol and unsnapped the thumb strap. My left hand reached for George's pistol and I twisted George's hand to the outside to break his grip on the gun. I felt my pistol catch on the thumb guard as I pulled it from the holster. Since I was so close to George, I wanted to end this quickly, so I thought that I would place the barrel of the Sig under George's chin and fire. This would end the struggle immediately and then I could deal with the other two men. At the very moment that I twisted the gun out of his hand, I observed that the pistol did not have a magazine in it. This realization zapped though my mind just as my finger started pulling the trigger.

I stepped back with George's pistol in my left hand and my pistol pointing at him. I ordered all the men to stand still. I then saw the eyes of the little boys. They were bigger than saucers. I told them to stay where they were. George suddenly broke into tears and started crying.

He kept repeating, "I only wanted to show it to you; I only wanted to show it to you."

I couldn't believe he was saying this to me. He had given me no warning that he was going to take the pistol out of its holster, and then had pointed it at me. I felt so lucky that my adrenaline had kicked in and that the whole world slowed down into nanoseconds. I also felt good that all the years of practicing defensive tactics had paid off as I was able to instinctively twist the pistol out of his hand. This George was one lucky, albeit, stupid guy. I don't think he had any idea how close he came to getting a .40 cal. bullet driven though his brain.

After I searched the other men and checked their rifles I took George up to my truck to talk with him and get some identification.

George's eyes were still teary and he spoke quickly. He kept apologizing for having pointed his gun at me. He said that he had just gone through a hunter's safety course and knew better. He again said he had just wanted to show me the pistol. I explained to him how close he had come to being killed and it was only that I had had excellent training and was an experienced law enforcement officer that he was alive at this moment. He said he knew that and thanked me. He said that he was going to sell the gun as soon as he could since he didn't have the ability to handle it.

I went back down the wash and talked with the boys to reassure them that everything was alright. George's son asked me if I was going to shoot his Dad. I told him that only a second of judgment prevented that from happening.

At the end we all shook hands and I left the scene. As drove away I could feel the adrenaline draining out of my body and I thanked God for watching over both George and me.

CH🌲PTER SEVENTEEN
NOT TODAY

California Desert District, Palm Springs, CA

I had gotten up early that morning. It was my first day back at work after my mother's death and I wanted to get into my regular work routine. I had called Border Patrol the night before and found out that all the Border Patrol checkpoints were operational across Imperial and Riverside Counties. This meant that the illegal alien smugglers or "coyotes," as they were known, would be transporting groups of illegal aliens across the Chocolate Mountain Bombing Range and onto BLM land.

The Chocolate Mountain Bombing Range is an active range used by the military and it also has an active Navy SEAL Base within its boundaries. There are no fences to keep people out, only sun-faded signs. The Chocolate Mountains basically ran north-west to southeast for approximately 50 miles between Highways 111 and 95. There are numerous old mining and military roads traversing the range. When the Border Patrol checkpoints are operational, the bombing range becomes the main route for human traffickers. The "coyotes" have no regard for the safety of their illegal clients, transporting groups as large as seventy-five people with the going rate of $1,500 per person to get to Los Angeles. To them, losing a few illegal aliens to the hazards of the range is all in the cost of doing business.

The sun was just rising as I turned off Interstate 10 about 3 miles east of the Red Cloud exit. This is where the El Paso gas line crosses the freeway and heads south towards El Centro. There was supposed to be a locked gate at this point in the freeway fence, but so many smugglers had crashed though it the highway department stopped repairing it. As I drove south along the Gasline Road, I didn't see any fresh tracks on the road. About 3 miles down the road I noticed some ironwood branches that just didn't look natural. I stopped my vehicle and walked about 50 feet over to them. There under the freshly cut branches I found 20 one-gallon jugs of water. None of the jugs had been opened and they all had fresh expiration dates on them. It had been three weeks since I was in this area, so I knew this cache was pretty new and it confirmed what I believed was going on. Since the checkpoints were operational, the traffickers were now using this route. Most traffickers used vehicles to bring their human cargo across the range, but about a third of the "coyotes" walked their groups the 30 miles from the safe houses in Niland. This was one of their water stops.

I left the jugs in place and continued south. I drove slowly watching for fresh tracks. I didn't see anything until I crossed over the boundary for the bombing range. Suddenly, there in the dry dust were numerous tracks. I got out of my vehicle and walked back to where the tracks left the road. I saw where the group had stopped and stood around. Apparently they had seen me before I had seen them. From the number of footprints this was a large group. I radioed my location to dispatch and got Jody heading my way. I grabbed my binoculars and followed the tracks. As soon as I got to the first wash I saw a group of five illegals running away from me. As I jogged behind them the group became larger and larger until I had over thirty illegals ahead of me. It was like jumping a covey of quail. At this point I was about a mile from my vehicle and I had only two sets of handcuffs with me. I decided the odds were not in my favor. I had often caught groups of five or ten illegals by myself, but thirty seemed like a lot and I didn't know how many others were out there. I radioed back to dispatch and requested Border Patrol to send additional units. I also had them call the bombing range to stop any range activity and walked back to my vehicle.

About a quarter mile from my vehicle I observed a person laying in a wash. I saw that the person was an Hispanic male in his twenties. I drew my Sig Sauer pistol and ordered him in Spanish to raise his hands. I got no response. I started to think this might be a trap to draw me in closer, so I made a large circle around him making sure that there was no one else in the area. I ended up standing behind him. If he tried to lunge at me he would have to turn around which would have given me some reaction time. He still didn't respond to my requests. He appeared to be unconscious. I could see that he was breathing rapidly. I holstered my gun and touched his forehead. His skin was hot and dry. Even though it was only about nine o'clock in the morning, the temperature was already close to 100 degrees. I could tell that he was suffering from dehydration and was probably somewhere between heat exhaustion and heat stroke.

He finally opened his eyes and looked at me. He repeated, "Aqua, aqua." I tried to communicate, but my Spanish was no better than his English. I finally got him to stand and walk toward my vehicle. We walked about 10 feet and he fell down. He lay on the ground completely unresponsive. I couldn't drive my vehicle to him because of the deep cuts in the wash, so I carried him. I was able to get him to partially stand up and then I bent down and placed him in a fireman's carry over my shoulder. He weighed about 150 pounds. If I put him down I'd never be able to get him up on my shoulder again. By the time we reached the vehicle I was completely drenched in sweat, but we made it.

I laid him down and placed an insulated pad under him so he wasn't lying on the hot ground. I then made a small lean-to with a tarp to keep the sun off. I wet his shirt with water and I placed a cool pack of ice under each armpit. The brachial artery is close to the surface in the armpits and I knew this would help to cool him. His pulse was weak and rapid. I transmitted all this information to dispatch and requested a helicopter to evacuate him. I was told that neither the California Highway Patrol helicopter nor hospital helicopter would fly to my location because we were on the bombing range. Dispatch was finally able to get a paramedic from Niland to respond. Since I knew there were at least thirty other people who might be close to the same condition as this man, I requested that Border Patrol send at least two BORSTAR (Border Patrol Search, Trauma and Rescue) units.

He went in and out of conscious for the next hour and a half. I tried to cool him down and keep him comfortable. After burying my mother a week previously, I just didn't want someone else to die on me my first day back at work. Finally, the paramedic from Niland arrived and he administered an IV-solution to replace the fluids that the man had lost.

At about this time, the BORSTAR units arrived along with Jody, Lisa, and Wes. Circling the area just outside the bombing range was H-63 the California Highway Patrol airplane. Since I knew where the illegal aliens were last seen, I returned to that location and started tracking. The other units patrolled both the Bradshaw Trail and Gasline Road. Wes brought a quad with him so I sent him about 5 miles north of our location to look for tracks on all the small trails that crossed the area. The group had about a two-hour head start on us, but I knew that the heat and the sound of the aircraft would keep the group moving slowly.

I put on my tactical vest with plenty of water and quickly located individual tracks. As I figured the group had reformed after the point that I had turned back. The tracks showed that groups of two or three persons joining together into larger groups until they all were one large group heading north towards the water cache. Wes suddenly came on the radio and said that he could see a group of five illegals walking parallel to the Gasline Road. He then saw four or five more groups for a total of 28 illegal aliens. H-63 went to Wes' location and the pilot said he could see two persons carrying another between them. The BORSTAR units immediately responded to the scene and were able to locate the three. Two males were carrying a fourteen-year-old female. She suffered from dehydration. The BORSTAR crew immediately started administrating fluids to her.

As the rest of the group was given water and food, the Border Patrol agents interviewed them. The 32 illegal aliens were dropped off by "coyotes" just north of the SEAL base on Gasline Road. They had been given no water or food and had been told to walk north along the road until they reached Interstate 10 where another "coyote" waited for them. They did not know the distance was about 30 miles. When I found them they had been walking for about ten hours and had covered about 20 miles. The first man I found had been having trouble for the past 3 hours. Others in the group also started to experience fatigue, dehydration, and other problems. My arrival had scared the group enough to give them a quick adrenaline hit to get them moving, but it soon wore off. Despite serious health risks the group continued moving north, driven by the desire to work in the United States.

With air temperatures over 100 degrees, I'm sure the whole

group would not have made it to the water cache or the Interstate, and I know the man I found would not have made it. I'm glad that my returning back to work that day had made a difference, and at least no one had to die.

CH🌲PTER EIGHTEEN
ABOVE THE ARCTIC CIRCLE

Fairbanks District, Coldfoot, AK

One of the more interesting details I worked for BLM, was a thirty-day assignment to Coldfoot Alaska in 1998. Coldfoot is located in the Brooks Range about 35 miles north of the Arctic Circle and is the halfway point between Fairbanks and Prudhoe Bay on the Alaskan Pipeline Highway. Coldfoot consists of a truck stop, motel, and little else. My job was to patrol the BLM lands along the pipeline—all 450 miles. My main duties were contacting the local gold miners and checking up on the many illegal tour operations which were conducted along the highway.

Upon my arrival, I found out that the cabin I was supposed to stay in was being used by someone else. So I got stuck in a small 24-foot trailer with no electricity or running water. I had a pit toilet outside the trailer made of three sheets of plywood with the opening facing away from the trailer. Electricity wasn't really an issue because it was daylight twenty-four hours a day.

My first "night" in the trailer I was awakened by what I thought was an earthquake. Having grown up in Southern California I felt for sure that I was in the middle of at least a 5.0 quake. When the quake stopped I walked outside and the first thing I saw was a large grizzly bear walking down the road. As the bear walked away I could see his muddy tracks leading away from the trailer. I walked to the front of the trailer and there on the front hitch I saw a large pile of hair and bear tracks all around. The grizzly bear had decided to use the hitch as a scratching post and that earthquake I thought I had felt was the bear pushing against the trailer. I truly was in Alaska! The rest of my stay there, I always looked out my window before I walked to my patrol truck, and I never used the pit toilet without having my shotgun with me.

Even today, large caribou herds cross the pipeline highway in many places. Hunting was not allowed within a mile of the pipeline. On opening day of bow hunting season two of the resident rangers took me on a patrol of the tundra area north of Galbraith Lake to look for hunters within the one-mile corridor. We each had a quad and started out together. After about an hour we were separated by about a quarter mile, and suddenly the area became completely fogged in. I couldn't see more than 100 feet in front of me. I completely lost sight of both the rangers. I knew that I was about 3 miles from where we left the trucks, and I had been driving parallel to the base of the Brooks Range when the fog came in. So I figured if I drove south I should run into the Brooks Range and then I could follow the drainage back to the trucks.

Ideas like these always sound great when you first figure them out, but as you execute them doubts start to form. I kept driving south but I didn't run into the mountains. I thought about turning around, but then I decided that was a bad idea. I kept thinking that before the fog overtook me the Brooks Range was to the south of me.

After about two hours I finally ran into the Brooks Range and followed the drainage back to the trucks. There were my two fellow rangers sitting on the tailgate of the trucks waiting for me. Both of them had big smiles on their faces. They had GPS units which were set for the trucks and had easily found their way back when the fog closed in.

They said they could hear my quad for the last hour, so they weren't too worried about me. They just thought it would be pretty funny if the southern California boy had disappeared into the wilds of the Alaskan tundra. The dark ranger humor knows no bounds.

I made a lot of contacts with the local gold miners. These men and women were all true individuals with a strong drive of self-purpose. They were hard workers that believed they should be left alone to do their mining on public lands without any restrictions from the federal government. They felt that since they were working the land it belonged to them not to the rest of the American people. It was always interesting trying to explain that they only had the mineral rights to their small claims and didn't have the right to exclude other people from the land or misuse it with their dozers and chemicals.

One of the wonderful things that I experienced in Alaska was the helpfulness and concern that Alaskan people feel for each other. Everyone seems to know what a fine edge they live on in Alaska. Even though I didn't belong to the most popular group in Alaska, I experienced the helpfulness of the people when the gas tank fell off my truck about 60 miles north of the Yukon River.

Here's a little lesson for rangers out there, when you go on detail and don't bring your own patrol vehicle, you're not going to get the best rig in the fleet, it just doesn't happen. I was given a Dodge truck that had over a hundred thousand miles on it. It was due to be turned in before I got there, but they had brought it out of storage for me. There were a lot of things wrong with it, but it met my basic standards. It stopped and started on command.

As I drove north of the Yukon River in the middle of a rainstorm I heard a loud crash and the sound of something dragging. I stopped the truck and looked under the carriage. There, sitting on the muddy road was my gas tank attached to the truck by only the small gas line. The two straps around the gas tank had broken causing the tank to drop.

I had no radio and no phone service, and knew I had to fix this myself. I thought about what I was going to do as I waited for the rain to stop. I had some small tie downs in the truck and a piston jack. I thought I might be able to lift the tank with the jack and then use the tie downs to secure the tank.

The rain stopped and I started to fix my problem. I could get the tank up off the roadway, but it was too big for one person to lift all the way into place. I tried for about an hour, but I just couldn't do it myself. Finally a trucker came by and asked if I needed help. By this time I was completely covered in mud and wasn't too happy. Without any hesitation he got down from his rig, put on his coveralls and climbed under my truck.

The two of us were able to secure the tank and he suggested that I stop at the Jim River Pumping Station and see if they had a bigger strap. I thanked him and drove slowly to the pumping station. There a mechanic put my truck on a lift and placed two large straps around the gas tank securing it better than it ever had been. I thanked him and was able to patrol for over a week before the right straps were available in Fairbanks.

On my way back to Coldfoot I dropped off a case of beer for the mechanic at the pumping station. He seemed surprised that I would think I needed to repay him. He said that people in Alaska just help one another, payment was not expected.

CHAPTER NINETEEN
SOMETIMES WHEN YOU VISIT HELL, YOU GET BURNT
California Desert District, El Centro, CA

Glamis or the official name, the Imperial Sand Dunes Recreation Area, is made up of the Algodones Dunes which runs northwest from below the Mexican border to the base of the Chocolate Mountains in the southeast corner of California. The dunes are picturesque in their composition, looking like everyone's view of a sand-driven desert scene. The dunes blocked the early settlers in their move west, but by the 1960s it had become the weekend haven for the sand buggy crowds from San Diego and Los Angeles who raced their flathead motorized rigs across the dunes. As the years progressed, the sand buggies became super charged sand rails and a whole lifestyle grew out of going to Glamis. By the early 90s, when I first arrived at Glamis, more than three hundred thousand people would visit on a holiday weekend.

As Glamis grew, the Bureau of Land Management did not keep pace with the increasing larger crowds. There were times when I worked the evening shift with only five other law enforcement rangers. Along with having to perform our regular law enforcement duties we also had to provide emergency medical services. Many times I can remember being all by myself, surrounded by a large drunken crowd trying to arrest someone who had just done some stupid drunken thing and wondering if I would get out of there in one piece. I was always thankful that even a drunk can find a special place in his heart for a ranger. Without a strong law enforcement presence Glamis got the reputation as a wide open area where you could do pretty much what ever you wanted to with little consequences for your actions.

Glamis was a dirty little secret to most of the upper level managers of the BLM. Managers liked to have sun shining skies around them and the law enforcement problems of Glamis certainly brought some dark clouds into view.

The BLM state and local law enforcement programs were supervised by managers who had no law enforcement experience. Their law enforcement views were formed by the last episode of COPS they watched, or their liberal biases from their college days. I don't know how many meetings I attended where some manager after being told about an incident, would frame his response by what he had seen on some fictional law enforcement show on television.

Finally the deaths and complaints became too much. It was decided that some action must be taken. The decision was to bring in more rangers from around the state to increase our presence and bring some order to Glamis.

Competition Hill or Comp Hill was the main focal point for most of the lawless behavior. Comp Hill was comprised of a large bowl about 10 acres in diameter situated at the base of a large dune. Generations of drivers have tested their machines and skills trying to climb that hill. Many people parked in the bowl just to watch the action. No paved roads went into the bowl which limited our patrol of the area. The crowds that we saw gathered were more interested in partying than watching the hill climbing.

Quads and sand rails were stolen on a regular basis. Numerous fights occurred in the area, along with underage drinking and drug use. Bob, the El Centro Chief Ranger, decided that this would be a good place to start to bring some order to the area.

Bob was and still is one of the least transparent people I have known in my life. He is a devoted religious and family man. You always knew where you stood with Bob, so when he came up with the idea to go after the heart of the problem, the idea didn't feel as crazy as it really was. Even though we had more rangers this time it still meant that eight of us were going to drive into Comp Hill after dark and walk among a crowd of ten thousand people trying to bring order to an area that didn't really want it. Bob's plan definitely sounded crazy, but it also sounded like a great adventure.

We arrived after sunset and parked on a ridgeline on the east side of the bowl. The vehicles were parked in a semicircle with them all facing downhill. Bob had a very dry sense of humor so when he called this place the Little Bighorn, some of us smiled. The plan was to walk among the crowd, showing the flag and knowing it wouldn't take long for something to happen.

Right away we observed two young men wrestling in the sand. We walked over to see if it was really a fight or just two guys testing each other. It turned out that it was just two drunks wrestling. Since no one was hurt and there were no complaints from either side we decided to move on. Just as we were leaving, I looked to the right and saw my best friend, John, showing the biggest guy how to look for lizards under the sand. John had the guy with one of his arms behind his back and his head in the sand. Tom was immediately at John's side and they handcuffed him.

As John told the story the kid named Hogan, had tried to rush John attempting to knock him to the ground. John wrestled in high school and still knew the moves. He had deftly countered Hogan's attack. John had Hogan's arm behind his back before he knew what had happened. Hogan was about six-foot three and weighed 240 pounds. John stands five-foot nine and weighs about 170 pounds, so we were all impressed with John. Weeks later we gave John an imitation World Wrestling Championship belt for his quick work on the great hulk Hogan.

I got my vehicle and placed Hogan inside the cage. I could smell the strong odor of alcohol on his breath and the look on his face told me that he wasn't feeling too good. I arranged for an Imperial County Correction Officer to pick up Hogan at the top of Comp Hill where Highway 78 is close to the sand. When I got to the location I opened the back door and told Hogan to turn his face away from me as I took off his seat belt. I had been spit on and thrown up on too many times not to be cautious. Just as I got the seat belt off him, I heard the wench as he vomited all over my jacket and himself. Not good! Besides the fact that there was vomit on myself, my vehicle and Hogan, I knew that the correction officer would never transport him in this state and I certainly didn't want to drive the 50 miles to El Centro smelling vomit all the way. John and I quickly got Hogan out of the vehicle and washed him off with the emergency water canteens that I carried. Now we had a wet drunk, but we knew that the correction officer would take him. As we waited for the correction officer, who was delayed, Hogan got colder and colder in the night air and started shaking. Now we had a wet, cold drunk. We were able to borrow some wool blankets from another unit and get him warmed up. Finally the transport unit arrived and we were both grateful when Hogan was placed in the Imperial County unit and driven off to El Centro.

As we arrived back at Little Bighorn a driver of a high-powered electric cart drove up to us and stated that he had picked up an intoxicated woman who was seated next to him. He found the woman wandering around the base of Comp Hill and had tried to help her find her group of friends. The woman was quite beautiful.

The driver was at least one hundred pounds overweight with triple chins. He was concerned for the woman's safety and I think he was looking for permission to take her back to his camp. I spoke to the woman and even though she had been drinking she did know where she was and where her camp was located. She stated she could take care of herself and it appeared that she could. She got out of the cart and walked away. The fat driver voiced his concerns about her and seemed a little disappointed that she had left him. I told him that she knew what she was doing and that when you visit hell there's always a chance that you might get burnt.

John and I found Bob just as he was returning to the vehicles. By this time the bowl was completely filled with vehicles and people. There were no roadways or passage ways through the crowd. Raging bonfires circled the area. The smell of smoke, gasoline, and dust choked the air; and the roar of man-made machines pierced the night.

As we talked, a blue Toyota 4runner pulled up in front of us and a man and women exited the vehicle. The woman was in tears and the man spoke in short choppy sentences. You could see the scared faces of their children looking out the windows. They had been trying to find a way out when they thought they had found a passage. It had turned out to be a trap. They had driven over gas-soaked sand that had been lit under them as they passed. As the flames died down, the crowd had ripped off their antennas and rocked the vehicle back and forth. The man had been able to speed up his vehicle and get away. All they wanted now was a safe place to hide. Again the thought ran through my head about what happens to people when they visit hell.

Bob got us organized and the eight of us went to investigate. It didn't take long to find the passageway and the flames. We watched as a man dressed in a plastic face mask danced around the passageway with a can of gas. He dug a trench in the sand poured gasoline in and covered it up. As a vehicle passed over the site he would ignite the vapors rising from the sand causing a flash explosion. Then the crowd would rock the vehicle back and forth or throw beer cans at it. We watched this happen two more times as we worked our way closer. We knew we had the masked man for endangerment and probably for enticing a crowd.

Bob decided that he and I would grab the masked man and the other rangers would protect our retreat back to the Little Bighorn. Everything went well as Bob and I both grabbed an arm of the masked man. We started heading up to the vehicles when all hell broke loose. Beer bottles and cans started flying through the air at us. You could hear them passing by and feel the spray. The only good thing was that they weren't hitting us. They were hitting other people in the crowd. I watched as two people took cans directly to the face and another women got knocked completely off her quad by the impact of a beer bottle to her chest. This drove the crowd back from us. It was like the parting of the Red Sea. We got about 50 feet then I could hear a rising chant coming from the crowd, "Kill the rangers, kill the rangers."

I looked around and there was Reid Hopkins with his law enforcement dog, Paco, holding back the crowd. Paco stood on his rear legs baring its teeth and barking furiously. The image of Reid and Paco standing there alone, holding back the crowd will always be etched in my mind. A brave man and his dog doing their duty, doing what they had been trained to do: protect their fellow rangers.

I looked at Bob and asked if he thought we should turn around. We both knew that Reid and Paco could take care of themselves so we headed towards the vehicles. Just as I had taken my first steps, a full beer can, a Coors Silver Bullet, hit me in the head at the base of my skull. A sudden flash of white pierced my mind and I could feel my legs buckle, but I stayed upright. Bob asked me if I was alright. I could feel a liquid running down my neck and I wasn't sure if it was blood. I rubbed my hand on it but in the darkness I couldn't tell. I tasted it and it was beer. I told Bob I was alright.

We made it back to the vehicles just as the crowd surged around us. Reid and the other rangers had also made an orderly retreat back to our location. The crowd had now grown to about two thousand people with the chant, "Kill the rangers," still echoing strong. We decided to form a line in front of the main body of the crowd. We had nowhere else to go. So this was where we would make our stand. Someone questioned Bob's naming this place the Little Bighorn. We drew our collapsible PR-24 batons and sapped them into their full length. The sap of a PR-24 is not as impressive as the rack of a round into a Remington 870 shotgun, but it still gets people's attention. We were able to push the crowd back a little ways and Reid and Paco walked the line keeping the crowd away.

Just as we got the crowd separated I could see that something was happening towards the back. The commotion continued forward until it reached the front. I thought someone was trying to power their way into our line. Then I realized that it was two BLM special agents and a group of undercover agents from the San Diego County Sheriff office. They had been working undercover and when they had seen what was happening they singled out the leaders in the crowd. Now they had grabbed three of the leaders and were bringing them to our side of the line. The crowd responded with throwing beer cans, but little else. This action appeared to take a little wind out of the crowd. We were able to increase the distance between the crowd and us to about

10 feet. This had the affect of creating a passageway for vehicles and we soon had an effective barrier between us and the crowd.

The agents were able to get the four suspects out of the area in unmarked vehicles. After about an hour the crowd started to dissipate. We still had a few cans being thrown at us, but things were settling down. We were all tired after the night's activities, especially as the adrenaline drained out of our bodies. None of us wanted to leave even though there was little else we could do. We had made a stand at Comp Hill for the first time and we didn't want to look like we were being forced out of the area until we were ready.

Due to this incident and others, the managers were forced to take a harder look at what was happening at Glamis. Suddenly statements of support were being made and managers that had never set foot at Glamis appeared on sight. The dirty little secret was appearing on the pages of the Los Angeles Times and the San Diego Union Tribune and the managers now had to deal with some clouds across their sunny little skies.

CH🌲PTER TWENTY
A JOURNEY INTERRUPTED

Ironwood Forest National Monument, Tucson, AZ

The large cumulonimbus clouds had been building all afternoon as Wes and I followed the footprints across the Roskruge Mountains. The large anvil head reached over us and the monsoon rains started falling. Soon the tracks were washed away and the road and the surrounding desert were covered with flowing water. To this day there is nothing in my mind more magnificent than a summer monsoon rainstorm on the upper Sonoran Desert. The intensity of these storms is awesome. The way they build up, release their energy, and then disappear is one of nature's great moments.

Wes and I watched the storm pass over us and then started back towards Silverbell Road about 20 miles away. We were on a two-week special detail to catch illegal aliens crossing from the Tohono O'odham Indian Reservation onto the Ironwood Forest National Monument in southern Arizona. Border Patrol had limited agents in this area and the environmental damage and destruction of natural resources due to human trafficking had gotten out of hand. The constant human presence threatened to eliminate the wildlife. Soil compaction along the roads and footpaths had become such a problem that the shallow root systems of the towering saguaro cactus were compressed, causing the saguaros to topple over taking with them animal food sources and bird nests. Arizona Game and Fish water tanks were being used by humans for drinking, meanwhile denying desert wildlife a drinking resource. Tons of trash was left behind as the illegal aliens waited under shade trees to be picked up. The local rangers just could not keep up with the influx of traffic. The idea was that by bringing more rangers into the area, we might be able to direct the traffic away from the monument.

As we drove back along the two track roads bordering the Tohono O'odham Reservation, the dry arroyos began to flow with rain water. The first two arroyos presented no problems. As we crossed the third arroyo it appeared no different from the others. The water was a little deeper, but nothing that a Ford F-250 four-wheel drive truck couldn't handle. But as we started to ascend out of the wash, the truck jerked to a stop. Wes backed the truck up and tried again. The same thing happened, but this time the truck slid sideways, pushed by the current. I looked out the passenger side window and could see the water pushing against the door about halfway up to the window. This was not a good thing! I yelled to Wes to put down the windows. Wes gunned the engine and was able to get the truck's front wheels out of the water, but now the rear bed of the truck was filled with water.

I could see a large palo verde tree just to the side of the road above the arroyo. I figured if I could make it to the tree I could get the winch cable around the tree and if we couldn't pull the truck out of the arroyo at least it wouldn't get washed away. I only had a year before I was going to retire and I didn't particularly want the last thing that people would remember me for was that I got a truck washed away.

I got the winch control cable from under the front seat and took off my weapon belt. I couldn't open the door because the water was pushing against it. I crawled out the window and on to the hood of the truck and then jumped to the road. I attached the control cable to the winch and pulled the cable off the spool and around the tree. Amazingly, the truck's engine was still running even though the exhaust pipe was underwater. With the winch I was able to pull the truck a little more out of the water and Wes was able to drive to truck out of the wash. Water rushed out of the bed of the truck.

As quick as the water had come up, it went down again. As the road was exposed we could see that the water had cut the steep bank into the road bed. This had caused the truck to stop and had been the reason why Wes hadn't been able to drive out of the wash. Wes and I both knew better than to cross an arroyo with water flowing in it. We had made a rookie mistake. Wes and I just looked at each other and then got big shit-eating grins on our faces. We had made a mistake, but had gotten out of it by the skin of our teeth.

By the time we got back to our observation point below Waterman Peak, it was almost dark. From this area we could watch the junction of three roads and observe vehicles exiting the reservation. We had just finished dinner when we heard the rattle of a vehicle approaching our location. The sound just wasn't right. We realized that the vehicle wasn't coming off the reservation, but was heading towards it. The vehicle was traveling at a high rate of speed and had its headlights turned off. Since such actions were creating a hazard, we decided to stop the vehicle and find out what was going on. As soon as we came out of our hiding spot and got behind the vehicle, the driver accelerated. On the twisting road it didn't take long before the driver lost control of the vehicle and slid off the road and into a ditch.

The driver immediately jumped out of the truck and ran into the desert. I stopped my vehicle and ran after him. It didn't take me long to give up the chase. The ground was rocky with little soil and it was a moonless night, so I had nothing to follow or track by. I returned to the truck where Wes was searching the vehicle. Inside he found three roasted chickens, four packages of tortillas, a case of Pepsis and five gallons of drinking water. The chickens were warm having just been purchased at a local grocery store just 10 miles from here. The receipt was time dated just forty-five minutes before. We had run into a smuggler going to pick up a load of illegal aliens. We found a cell phone charger in the truck so we figured the driver probably would place a warning call to his boss about not using this area. But we also knew that cell phone coverage was not that good in this spot so we might get some action later in the evening. We went back to our observation point and waited.

About 10:45 p.m. we saw headlights reflecting against the mountains as a vehicle exited the reservation. It was apparent that word had not reached this group of smugglers that we were in the area. We watched as the truck approached the junction of the road and then stopped. Through our night vision goggles we saw that the bed of the truck held at least fifteen illegal aliens, and we could hear the driver talking to someone. The truck then turned east. We had taken the law enforcement Honda 400 quad out of Wes' truck earlier in the evening and had hidden his truck farther up the road. The plan was for Wes to make the stop and I would back him up in my vehicle. If the smugglers tried to run, Wes would be able to stay with them on the quad.

As soon as Wes turned on his red lights, the truck immediately started to accelerate and then turned off its headlights. This area had not received as much rain so the road was dusty. The dust slowed us as we tried to stay up with the truck. Suddenly, there was no dust on the road and no truck, so we knew the truck had turned off into the desert. Wes made a fast U-turn and I followed. About a quarter mile back I could see Wes drive off the road and into the desert. As my headlights shone on him, I could see Wes standing with his AR-15 rifle pointed towards the truck. People were jumping off in all directions. I pulled up on the opposite side of Wes and lit the whole area up with the vehicle spotlight.

In our broken Spanish we ordered the illegal aliens out of the vehicle and rounded up the few that were trying to run. We had a total of 19 people, 5 women and 14 men. We got everyone away from the truck and seated them along the road. We searched just one and looked through their packs. This was an extremely well organized group. All had the basic same type of day packs with personnel items kept in zip lock bags. They carried no water or identification. This group had been prepared to be taken to a pickup point along Silverbell Road and then moved to Phoenix or Los Angeles. They had already completed their 50-mile walk from the border.

After searching everyone, we handed out water and crackers. This always seemed to calm everyone down. After an adrenaline charge you're always hungry and thirsty. I notified Border Patrol of our location and then went to search the truck. On the driver's side floor mat I found a fully-loaded Barrette 9 mm pistol. Apparently the driver had dropped it as he exited the vehicle. I called the serial numbers into dispatch and they told me the pistol had been reported stolen out of Phoenix. When Wes and I got to the truck no one was standing at the driver's side of the vehicle, and of course, none of the illegal aliens admitted to owning this gun.

After waiting two hours for Border Patrol to arrive, we had our dispatch check about their estimated time of arrival. We were told that two vans had tried to find us, but had turned back because of shift change. After some more checking we were told that one

Border Patrol agent was trying to find us. He did not know the area that well, but did know about the junction below Waterman Peak. Wes and I decided to walk this group back to the junction which was about a mile away. We finally arrived at the junction just as Border Patrol pulled up. The agent was able to get everyone into his van and we escorted him back to Silverbell Road. Wes and I finally made it back to the motel just as the sun was rising.

CH🌲PTER TWENTY-ONE
THIEF OF TIME

Elko District, Elko, NV

A strong series of thunderstorms had moved across northern Nevada igniting hundreds of lightning fires which burned over 740,000 acres of BLM land. I was given the assignment to work with the recovery team helping to protect the many newly exposed archeological and natural resource sites.

The Elko District of BLM was always an interesting place to work. It was the center of the Sagebrush Rebellion with some of the hardest anti-government hatred in the United States. As I drove into the district from the south, I found the wooden BLM district sign covered over with a banner that read, "Elko County Runs the Public Lands, Not the BLM."

It always amazed me how the local residents thought that just because they lived in areas where there were public lands, those lands belonged solely to them. I don't know how many times local persons would get into my face about how I shouldn't be there and that they and their grandfather's grandfather had lived in this area since Moses parted the seas, as the saying goes.

I always answered that the public lands belonged as much to them as it did to the little old lady in Rhode Island who may never even see this land in her whole life time. I told them that I and the BLM represented the interests of that lady and the 280 million other citizens of the United States to whom this land belonged. This response didn't usually sit well with the old-time ranchers and grazers. But I think in their hearts they knew the truth of my statements. As I looked at the sign I knew that my time in Elko would be interesting.

After being shown the area by Erika, I started patrolling the area by myself. During the first week I caught two people illegal dumping trash and cited a group of deer hunters for driving their vehicles into a wilderness area. I also ran into Ron Stein and his wife walking along the old California Trail north of Rock Springs. The trail was a branch of the Oregon Trail where over two hundred fifty thousand people had traveled on their way to the California Gold Rush. The trail had been covered by sagebrush for years, but the fires then exposed miles of the trail.

When I first saw Stein and his wife I thought they were sage grouse hunters. They had a beautiful German shorthair pointer with them and from a distance I thought they had shotguns in their hands. As I drove closer the shotguns turned out to be metal detectors. The California Trail is a national protected site and is closed to all archeological collecting; even metal detectors are not allowed in the area. By the time I reached the Steins, they had just reached their truck. The truck had a camper on it with a quad sitting on an attached trailer.

I asked Stein what he had been doing and he said just walking. His hands and the knees of his jeans were covered with ash. I asked if he knew he was walking along the California Trail. He said he thought it was somewhere in this area but didn't know exactly where it was. I explained to Stein that it was illegal to collect arti-facts along the trail and the use of metal detectors was specifically restricted. Stein again said he had only been taking a hike and liked carrying his metal detectors when he walked. He said he used it as a snake stick to protect his dog. Since neither Stein nor his wife had any artifacts on them I decided to give them a warning notice so I could get their identification and keep it for farther reference. As Stein opened his camper door to get his driver's license I could see topographic maps and guidebooks for the trail sitting on the table. I knew I had been lied to by Stein; my observations just confirmed it. I couldn't do much else at this point, but I knew I had someone to watch out for. Seven days and 125 miles later, heading south I met up with the Steins again. Late in the afternoon I decided to stop in the Mineral Hill area to check the archeological sites. Mineral Hill was an 1880s mining district which comprised of a small town with numerous mines surrounding it. The area had been completely burned to the ground exposing many of the old ruins. As I glassed the area with my binoculars, I saw a truck with a camper parked on the edge of some pinyon and junipers trees that hadn't been burnt. I recognized the truck as that belonging to Stein. I drove my patrol vehicle about a half mile from the Stein's campsite and walked to the vehicle. I wanted to surprise him this time. When I reached the truck, Stein wasn't there. The quad was off the trailer and the German shorthair pointer was tied to the truck. I moved my patrol truck closer and waited for Stein to return. I hid my vehicle where I could see his camper, but he couldn't see me.

It was almost dark when I heard the sound of Stein's quad approaching the camper. I could see Stein driving the quad with his wife riding behind. Two metal detectors were attached to the handle bars. When I contacted Stein he was extremely surprised to see me. I asked him to step off his quad and as he did I could see that he was wearing a pistol. There are no laws against wearing a pistol, so I just noted its presence. Again Stein's hands were covered with soot. As I talked with him, I could see that he was nervous especially after I found numerous rusty and soot-covered artifacts in a milk grate attached to the quad. He had a knife, part of a metal plate, a fork and a bullet mold in the grate.

Stein asked me if his wearing a pistol made me nervous. The way he said it I could tell he was trying to make a veiled threat. I looked him in the eye and said that I was pretty sure that I was better trained and quicker then he was so I wasn't too worried about him, and besides, if he killed me he'd be facing a lot worst charges than collecting artifacts.

Again Stein said he wasn't collecting, but when I pointed out his possession of the metal detectors, his soot covered hands, and the artifacts in the grate he finally admitted that he had collected the artifacts from all around the Mineral Hill area. He said he had been to the area before the fires. He had used the Internet to look at the BLM sites which showed the perimeters of the fires and when he saw that the fires had burned over the California Trail and the other archeological sites he had decided to return to the area and do some collecting. Based on his statements and what I found on the quad I decided that I had enough probable cause to search his camper. I didn't find any other artifacts, but I did find a computer print-out of the fire locations.

As I wrote Stein a citation, he just kept talking and talking about how this was so unfair. His whole argument for what he was doing was that if he didn't find these artifacts they would either rust away in the ground or be put in some museum drawer where no one would see them. Stein said he was going to give them to his grandchildren so that they would have something to remember him with. I asked him if he wanted to be remembered for being a thief, because that was exactly what he was doing, stealing from the American people and from time. Stein took his citation and later pleaded guilty and paid his fine.

CH🌲PTER TWENTY-TWO
A-CANAL WATER WARS

Klamath Basin, Klamath Falls, OR

A-Canal is one of the many irrigation canals feeding water to the fertile Klamath Basin in southeast Oregon. The irrigation system was completed in 1906 by the Bureau of Reclamation and the area was largely homesteaded by World War I veterans. The land and water was given to these veterans cheaply and they and their children worked hard to turn the land into a rich farming area. They paid a small fee to the government for use of the canal and water, but were smart enough never to actually acquire the ownership of the canal so that they retained the benefits of its use, but not the maintenance.

Everything went well for almost a century until the drought years of the late 90s which brought the water supply to critical levels. There was not enough water for both the farmers to irrigate, and for the Bureau of Reclamation to maintain sufficient flow levels so that salmon and other endangered species could be kept alive.

During the summer of 2001, the Bureau of Reclamation decided to decrease the flow of water through the A-Canal gates so that the salmon could survive in the river. The federal government, not the local farmers, had the right to regulate the water. Due to the abundance of water during the last century this had never been an issue. Now it became a matter of financial survival for those farmers using the federal water. Other farmers not part of the federal system had water to sell, but at a much higher price than federal water.

On July 4, 2001, the farmers took matters into their own hands and broke into the headgates and opened the valves so that the water flowed into the A-Canal. The local sheriff watched as the farmers trespassed on federal land, destroyed government property, and stole the water. The Bureau of Reclamation had contracted with the local sheriffs' office to provide protection for these and other facilities. The sheriff's decision to stand by and take no action gave the federal government no other choice than to bring in the US Marshal to restore control over the gates and protect the facilities. These actions drew the nation's attention.

The A-Canal became yet another rallying cry for the Sagebrush Rebellion advocates who felt that the public lands and water belonged to a select group of local users and not to the citizens of the whole nation.

After the US Marshals secured the headgates and it became clear that the local sheriff was not going to live up to his contract or uphold the law, a decision was made to use law enforcement officers from the Department of the Interior. The Bureau of Reclamation (BOR) is part of the Interior Department, but had neither law enforcement authority nor officers at that time. It was decided to have the US Fish and Wildlife Service oversee the operation with the BLM law enforcement rangers working as on-site enforcement personnel. BLM law enforcement rangers were in place by early August and had the gates guarded by August 23; then repairs were made and the water was again shut off. I had arrived the day before and stood guard as the large crowd sang songs and yelled insults at us. The crowd was separated from the headgates by a chain link fence and about 50 feet of ground owned by BOR. On the other side of the fence the protestors had erected a large tent. The tent was used for meetings and many people slept in it at night. The fence was festooned with anti-government signs and slogans.

Since BOR had no law enforcement authority and we couldn't use state laws, all the rangers were deputized as US Marshals. Under United States titles this gave us the limited right to protect property and ourselves. There were no laws we could use for trespassing. We stood between the protestors and the headgate with few laws behind us.

The day was filled with speeches and prayers against the federal government and the rangers in particular. We were accused of being "Redcoats" sent by Washington to oppress the farmers and their right to the water. The farmers demanded that the sheriff arrest us for trespassing. When questioned directly about whether he would arrest us he danced around the issue, keeping the crowd fired up.

There were some funny moments like when someone started a chant that went,

"What's a four letter word for a government employee S-U-C-K-E-R." We could never quite figure whether the crowd didn't know how to spell or how to count.

One group came up to the fence and demanded the return of an American flag that had been placed above the headgates when the farmers first took over. The flag had been flown upside down which is a sign for distress. When the marshals reclaimed the headgate, they flew the flag right side up. This maddened the crowd and they wanted their flag back. Since this was a minor issue the operations chief, Felicia, decided to give it back to them. Felicia let me handle taking down the flag and giving it to the protestors. Steve and I made a real ceremony of the event. We slowly took down the flag and folded it up into a perfect triangle with the stars facing outwards. I then took the flag and walked over to the fence looking for someone in the crowd that hadn't cursed or tried to spit on me. I found a middle-aged woman who looked reasonable. I then waited a second so the camera crews were all there, and gave her the flag. I told her that I was a disabled American veteran and I gave her the flag of our country with respect and that I expected that same respect. This action seemed to have a positive affect on the crowd. The insults lessened and the spitting stopped.

Towards the end of the day, the BOR agreed to let the protestors run a small pipeline around the headgates from the lake to the canal. The volume of water was insufficient, but the protestors were happy that they still had some water flowing into the canal. We got through the day without anyone climbing over the fence or trying to reclaim the headgate. No one had been hurt, but the lines had been drawn.

For the next five days the protestors were quiet. We got intelligence reports that the protestors gave the sheriff a deadline of 4:00 p.m., August 29 to remove the BLM Rangers or the farmers would take over the gates themselves.

On August 27, Felicia left and I was appointed operations chief. I felt the success of the operation had been placed on my shoulders. Neither the incident commander nor anyone above him was on scene. I was given two cell phones that rang constantly with people wanting to know what was going on and giving me "sage" advice. The deputy US Attorney's office called almost hourly with request from Washington wanting to know what was happening. Even Vice-President Dick Cheney's son-in-law called wanting information. The Republican administration didn't want to offend their Sage Brush Rebellion supporters, but they also didn't want an incident either, in their young administration. I felt quite alone knowing that if I succeeded there would be many taking the credit, but if I failed I would definitely be standing alone.

The other thing that went through my mind was that this was a chance to show that the Bureau of Land Management had a professional group of law enforcement rangers who were capable of handling a complex situation. I also knew in my heart that I was not going to let a local county sheriff place a Bureau of Land Management ranger under arrest. This would have destroyed years of federal law enforcement authority on public lands. Every small county sheriff in the West would have looked at it as a chance to dismiss federal authority over public lands. One of the first things I did when I became operations chief was to go around to each of the rangers and personally talk with them about the importance of being professional in our actions and my plan to resist all their attempts to arrest us. I got complete agreement from everyone.

On August 28, the protestors' numbers increased and the TV news satellite trucks returned. The circus atmosphere of the event grew. The protestors brought in ladders to scale the fence and hung numerous chains and locks from the fence. They yelled at us that the chains were for arresting us. One guy shouted that he was going to wrap me up in the chains and throw me in the canal. This time the crowd had state-rights protestors mixed in, including the Montana Militia known for its violent anti-federal leanings.

I received intelligence reports that one of the protestors named Joe was making statements that he would supply weapons to the protestors if they needed them. I was also told that Joe walked with a gnarled-handled cane which concealed a small sword inside the shaft of the cane.

Late in the afternoon the Klamath County sheriff held a meeting with me and USFW Agent Scott Pearson. He asked us to walk away from the headgates and leave the area. He said he had little control over the direction the crowd would take and was concerned with our safety. When I asked him if he was going to enforce the trespass laws that he had been contracted to enforce, he said he was still studying the ramifications of that act with the county district attorney. We told him we weren't leaving.

On the morning of the twenty-ninth, more protestors arrived and the main rally started at 4:00 p.m. For the first two hours, speeches were made against the sheriff for not arresting us, the federal government for its oppressive action against the farmers, and the constitutionally for the farmers actions. There were speeches urging reason and for working within the system, but they weren't as well received. The state-rights activists led by Arizona's former Sheriff Max kept the crowd aroused. At 6:00 p.m. Baron Knolls, a local farmer, placed the folding wooden ladder across the fence, climbed over and walked towards the headgates.

There were eight rangers to stop a crowd of approximately one-thousand people who wanted to arrest us and take over the headgate. I had Steve Fleming, Bill McDonald and John Weiner stand directly in front of the ramp which lead to the control valves. Scott stood directly in back of them and I stood in front of the whole group.

The crowd drew silent as Knolls approached us. I put my hand out and shook his hand and asked him how he was doing. He was surprised that I knew his name. I told him we knew everyone's name which was certainly a stretch of the truth, but I needed all the help I could get. Knolls handed me a list of the protestors' demands and asked that we'd step aside and let the protestors take over the gates. He promised that nothing would happen to us and we would be welcomed as true American heroes. I told Knolls I wouldn't do that and he said that didn't surprise him. He then asked if I was going to arrest him. I said I wasn't planning on doing that right now. The real reason I couldn't was there weren't any trespassing laws I could enforce, I had to bluff again. Only if the protestors attacked us directly or damaged property could we take any action.

When the crowd saw that Knolls wasn't being arrested people became emboldened. They climbed over the fence, first in ones and twos, then more and more. Soon, approximately two-hundred fifty people stood around us. For the next two hours groups of people came up to us saying that they were placing us under citizens arrest and asked us to follow them to the sheriff's office. Some were quite indignant when we didn't go with them. Others kept shouting insults. One man walked up to us with a clipboard and started writing down our names. He said he was going to destroy us financially. I looked over and saw that he had misspelled my name. I corrected his spelling and asked him if he needed anything else from me. This got a laugh from the crowd and the guy left.

Finally, the big moment came when an older man was brought up to the front of the crowd. I immediately recognized him as Joe, by the cane that he carried. Joe spoke to the crowd and told them that they were gutless for not pushing us aside and taking over the headgates. He then walked towards Marie Tuxhorn who had replaced Weiner in the line. I stepped in front of Joe and he literally bounced off me and started to fall backwards. His cane came up between my legs and struck my testicles. I don't think he meant to do that, but it really hurt. There was a moment that I thought Joe would fall down. I knew that wouldn't be good. Luckily someone caught him before he fell. That little incident seemed to have a positive effect for us. The crowd saw we weren't going to step aside and it shut Joe up. He was escorted away.

As it grew darker there was a gigantic hatch of midge flies which filled the air. These were tiny insects about the size of mosquitoes. They were attracted to the lights shining on the headgates. The midges became so dense you could hardly breathe without inhaling them. I was finally able to break the lamp above us which lessened the density of the midges. The crowd saw what I did and decided to bring back the insect attack. They pushed a portable light tower over to the head gate and started it. Immediately the midges returned, this time in greater numbers. Scott saw the problem and charged though the line and into the crowd. Scott was able to get to the light tower and started to disable it. At this point the crowd saw what he was doing and pulled Scott away. He returned to our line with a handful of wires and a disabled light tower. It was a brave act which was evident by the cuts on his arms.

This was the last major incident of the night. As it got later the crowd started to go home. We were still getting the insults and comments, but the momentum was ours. We had stood our ground and had not given up the headgates.

I had turned my cell phones off during the incident and when I turned them back on, all hell broke loose. Everyone wanted to know what had happened. The US Attorney's office and Washington were irate that I hadn't given them minute by minute updates of the past events. They calmed down a bit when they heard we had held the gates and no one had been hurt or injured. They wanted to know why I hadn't answered my phone. I told them that I was the one on the scene and that they had chosen to insulate themselves from the headgates. As the commander on scene these were my decisions to make and I didn't want to be second-guessed by someone sitting miles away. I didn't make friends with those statements, but I didn't care. We had done the job we had been sent to do.

The Director of the Bureau of Land Management ordered seventeen more rangers to back us up the next day. With the arrival of these rangers we now had enough rangers to protect the gates. The protestors moved their operation directly in front of the gates, but they made no other attempts to take back the gates. On September 2, US Fish and Wildlife agents took over guarding the area.

Since July 4, the protestors had conducted a hot and caustic war of wits with federal government over water rights. After September 11, 2001, with the United States in a real war with a foreign enemy, the Klamath Basin farmers decided to declare a truce. Citing love of country and undying patriotism, they removed their tents and protest signs and pulled up stakes. They stopped their unyielding rhetoric that made the A-Canal ground zero, that summer, for a push to reform the US Endangered Species Act and for Western water rights. In the aftermath of the terrorist attacks on the World Trade Center and Pentagon, the protestors said the time was wrong to go head to head with their own government and they stepped back.

CHAPTER TWENTY-THREE
THE LAST TIME

California Desert District, Palm Springs, CA

I got up early on the last day that I was a ranger, I wanted it to last as long as it could. I deliberately held out signing any papers till the last day, so I could patrol one last time. I loved being in my four wheel Tahoe driving the back roads patrolling.

I was on the road at 4 am and drove over Palen Pass and watched the sun came up over the McCoy Mountains. I had breakfast with Fred and Javier in Blythe and then started west on the Bradshaw Trail. It was a cold, rainy day, as most of that winter had been. The clouds along the Chuckwalla Bench reached almost to the ground. The clouds did not match my mood. Even though I knew this was my last patrol, all I could think about was how great it had been to have had this job. A few friends called as I drove across the Chuckwalla Bench. We reminisced about old adventures and good times.

I came upon the large mud hole that always formed along the road by Benton Tank. The road was covered for about one hundred yards with wet muddy water. This area was steeply banked so there was no going around it. I had pulled a few vehicles out of this hole before, so I knew it could eat them up. I thought about turning around for a second, but then decided against it. I backed up about a quarter mile and got a running start at it. I hit the hole at sixty miles per hour, mud flew everywhere. The wipers barely kept the windshield clear. As I got almost to the end of the hole, all four of my tires started spinning and the vehicle turned sideways. I straightened out the Tahoe and inched forwards. I knew if I stopped I'd never get the traction I needed to get out of the hole. As we inched forward, I finally felt the front wheels and then the rear wheels gain traction and we pulled onto solid ground.

I had taken a stupid little chance and gotten lucky one last time. I thought again about how many times I had taken much larger chances and had survived.

I got back to the office and washed the mud off the Tahoe. I went inside and signed all the final paperwork and turned in all my keys. Finally I took off my weapon belt, removed my shirt and unpinned the badge. I handed the badge to John and my career ended. For thirty years I had truly been one of the luckiest people in world to have been a ranger.

CH🌲PTER TWENTY-FOUR
PROLOGUE

I saved this last little admission for the end because it seemed like the right thing to do.

For the thirty years that I worked as a ranger, I was, and still am, an insulin-dependent diabetic. I learned quickly at Glacier that telling people you're a diabetic affects the way they view you and treat you. People become overly protective and allow their prejudices to limit what you're capable of doing.

When I became a diabetic at age twenty-one, while serving in the Army, I decided to control my disease the best I could and not allow it to control me. I did my job and didn't make a point of letting people know I was a diabetic. I always noted it on my yearly physicals, but never made point of advertising the fact. I only told my direct supervisors and my close friends.

I was lucky because when I got my first job with the Park Service and until 1994 there were no medical restrictions placed on diabetics doing law enforcement for the Department of the Interior. In 1994, those standards changed and persons with insulin-dependent diabetics were not allowed to do law enforcement. The department looked at the disease and not the person's ability to handle the disease. Since I was already a law enforcement ranger when the regulations changed, I was grandfathered into the program.

The real issue is how you control your diabetes. A person with good control of their diabetes is capable of doing anything that anyone else can do. I think I proved that over the last thirty years. So the next time you think someone with diabetes can't do something because of this disease, remember my stories.

CPSIA information can be obtained
at www.ICGtesting.com
Printed in the USA
BVHW081140130620
581307BV00003B/155

9 781583 851142